90 Minutes of Freedom

Prescoed FC.
The only prisoner football team in Wales.

Jamie Grundy

To Derek.

Footballer, team mate, coach, mentor, dad.

"Everything I know about morality and the obligations of men, I owe it to football."

Albert Camus

"The thing about football – the important thing about football – is that it is not just about football."

Terry Pratchett

Contents

1	Glossary	1
2	Foreword	3
3	Introduction	5
4	History Boys	9
5	Welcome to Prescoed	13
6	Sam	23
7	Tom	29
8	Bailey	33
9	Paul	41
10	Calum	45
11	Neil	49
12	John	55
13	Daniel	61
14	Jermaine	67
15	Joe	71
16	Alan	81
17	Chris	85
18	Undefeated	89
19	Final League Table, Season 2018/19	101
20	Acknowledgements	103
21	Notes	105

Glossary

Basic If you are on basic level Incentives and Earned Privileges it means you can have certain things that the law says you can have, like some letters and visits. You are not allowed anything extra.

Category B / B Cat A closed prison containing prisoners for whom the very highest conditions of security are not necessary but for whom escape must be made very difficult.

Category C / C Cat A closed prison for those who cannot be trusted in open conditions but who are unlikely to try to escape.

Category D / D Cat An open prison for those who can be reasonably trusted not to try to escape, and are given the privilege of an open prison.

CHASE Programme Collectively Heightening Awareness of Substance Misuse through Education programme at Prescoed, for men with substance misuse convictions.

Enhanced This means you can have even more extra things. For example, you may be allowed more visits, a TV in your cell, or to spend more of your money.

FAW Football Association of Wales.

Home leave A short period of temporary release from prison for up to seven nights per month, subject to statutory supervision on release.

HMPPS Her Majesty's Prison & Probation Service.

Induction Induction varies for prison to prison but all of them will cover the same ground: attend lectures and presentations about the prison rules and guidelines, what jobs or education opportunities exist, and details about visiting rules.

Lie down Describes the period of time when, if you are transferred to a prison of a lower category you are not normally be eligible for any ROTLs for three months, to allow for a new risk assessment to take place.

Lifer A prisoner serving a life sentence.

Listener	A peer support service which aims to reduce suicide and self-harm in prisons. Samaritans volunteers select, train and support prisoners to become Listeners, who provide confidential emotional support to their fellow inmates who are struggling to cope.
OMU	Offender Management Unit who work with the Offender Manager to help prisoners to complete certain goals of a sentence plan.
Orderly	A prisoner suitable for working within a trusted position within the prison.
NOMIS	National Offender Management Information System: the operational database used in prisons for the management of offenders. It contains offenders' personal details, type of offence(s), type of custody, sentence length, etc.
PEO	Physical Education Officer: a Prison Officer with a specialism for physical education.
Resettlement	The term used by prisons and probation services when you leave prison and go back into the community. Resettlement should mean that services support you and your family to prepare for life after prison.
ROTL	Release on Temporary Licence for a prisoner granted temporary release during their sentence. It is the mechanism that allows prisoners to participate in activities outside the prison that directly contribute to their resettlement into the community.
Stage One	Unpaid work placement for prisoners.
Stage Two	Paid work placement for prisoners.
Statutory supervision	The prisoner has to follow certain rules whilst in the community or they may be returned to custody.
YO	Young offender.
HMYOI / YOI	Her Majesty's Young Offenders Institution or Young Offenders Institution.

Foreword

Football is a sport that has always brought excitement and passion to anyone with a desire to play and get involved. Whether it is the winning or the losing, or even just the taking part, football has so much to offer beyond two goals and ball. '90 Minutes of Freedom' shows that, even when everything is taken from you, football is sometimes the only thing that remains.

Exercise has often been used to help people with their mental health and this is really true of football at Prescoed. Whether it is adapting to a strange new place with new people, learning how to keep your anger in check, coping with being away from your loved ones for months at a time, or dealing with post-traumatic stress disorder triggered by the horrors of war, football can help people to heal. What is clear from the experience at Prescoed is that football is being used in all these ways and more. The prisoners playing the game may not know it, but they are being prepared for a life beyond the prison walls and football offers them tools to reintegrate successfully into the community.

The real-life stories in this book show how football can help you cope with the most stressful of environments: being locked up and serving a prison sentence.

Neville Southall
September 2019

Introduction

This is a book about a Welsh prisoner football team, the only one in the country. If you love films like Mean Machine, Green Street, The Firm, ID, The Guvnor, Top Dog, Away Days or The Football Factory then I have some great news for you. I've just saved you the money and inconvenience of reading my book! This book is not like any of those. You're welcome.

Instead, this book is about what it means if you are a fair to middling footballer turning out for your local team on a Saturday afternoon with your mates. Except that your local team is a prisoner football team and you are a serving prisoner, as are your mates. It is made from interviews with the players who turned out for HMP Prescoed FC in South Wales in the Gwent Central Division Two for the 2018/19 season. It also includes an interview with one ex-player who played professionally before and after serving a prison sentence at Prescoed.

The book is inspired by my own experience of the late 1990s playing against teams from HMP Kirkham and HMP Wymott in Lancashire as a young, fair to middling footballer myself. In both cases, I was initially apprehensive and nervous about playing prisoners, but then soon realised that both teams contained players just like me, except they had made a mistake for which they were serving time. Since those formative years, I am now a professional working in the field of criminal justice, having worked on projects in each of the six Welsh prisons as well as one or two others in England, and I'm still playing football. During this time I have met many prisoners and had many conversations. A lot of them have involved talking about football either at my insistence or theirs, as something we've got in common and a way to break down barriers.

So having known that football is a good ice-breaker in a prison setting, I was intrigued to find out that HMP Prescoed had two grass football pitches. They were both hidden from the main prison camp and hidden from public view. I was working there for a few months co-ordinating an education course and wanted to know more because this is unheard of in prisons (grass pitches, not education of course). Plus, they also had a team who played in the local league. But when you searched for them online, only a very limited set of results were returned. The team and their pitches seemed to be a bit of an enigma.

At the same time, National Sporting Heritage were looking for community projects to support, to celebrate different forms of sports heritage. I suggested the opportunity to capture a moment or even a whole season in the time of a prisoner football team, to explore how sport has assisted rehabilitation efforts and the prisoners' plans for their future. Thankfully, they thought it was good idea and their support formed the impetus for this book. In some respects, this story isn't really about football; it is about sport as a tool for rehabilitation. This book aimed to offer a snapshot of the inside of a prison, a place rarely seen by many of us, but stories about crime, which we all hear and read about in the news every day, affect us all. I also wanted the voices of the prisoner footballers to be recorded and their views presented. They could talk about their experiences, their hopes and fears in their own words, not what someone else might think they are.

After getting the all clear the Ministry of Justice and the prison governor, I started turning up to each weekly training session and on a Saturday to get a feel for the team. Though the staff knew why I was there, I only let the players know as and when conversations started; but I was clear that I wanted to get to know the players, the team and the set-up first. The staff and the players were equally intrigued and supportive, though some players thought I was there to do a glossy magazine piece on each of them! I explained that not only was I not there from FourFourTwo, I would be using pseudonyms for each of them so that people could not tell who they were (a Ministry of Justice research requirement). But because I had got to know some of the players and their personalities, a sense of trust had been established and a good number of the players were interested in participating.

So I was there each week and I waited until the time was right to start interviewing the players. Then when I turned up one Saturday and it looked like Prescoed were going to be short of players, one of the players greeted me warmly with the words, "Get your fucking boots on Grundy, we're one short". At that point I knew I was in!

Players were interviewed one to one at all different times of the day, evening and weekend, according to their working, family or other prison commitments. They gave their voluntary informed consent, which means they agreed to participate, and each interview took place in a confidential interview room in the prison. The interviews were recorded, transcribed and then were checked by the prisoners themselves for accuracy. Only once they were happy with these interviews were they included in the book.

The sense of trust that had been built up was important and I feel it was present in the interviews. Although I was unable to verify all the facts or view any prison or offending details on them from NOMIS, I am confident that what they told me was representative of the truth. Whilst I acknowledge this may be considered by some to be a weakness of this book, the onus was very much on me to invest time being a part of the group. This is also a key aspect of ethnographical research, which involves observing and interacting with individuals in their real-life environment. Had I not spent time getting to know the team and the players, I would not be so confident. This approach was supported by the staff, who were candid in their assessment of some previous researchers, and who might have felt in the past that some people thought they can simply walk in and become an expert overnight. It takes time to get to know the players properly, sometimes longer than you think. But I hope it makes for a better book.

Throughout the season I was fortunate to be pitch-side and witness some excellent games of football, played by some unique footballers. I was able to share in the trials and tribulations of being an arms-length participant for most of Prescoed's games. Each week I was with the players in the changing room before and after games, ran the line, appealed for decisions, celebrated the goals scored and commiserated the goals conceded. I was as much a part of the group as I could be.

So these are the stories of the players and this is the story of HMP Prescoed FC, the only prisoner football team in Wales.

History Boys

Following the Second World War, according to the Home Office, there were only twenty-nine prisons housing more than 29,400 prisoners across England, Scotland, Wales and Ireland.[1] Today, there is a prison population usually around the 98,000 mark across one hundred and sixteen prisons.[2] During the War, the Home Office had understandably been pre-occupied with issues surrounding the hostilities. But following its end, in 1945, it started to look inward at rebuilding aspects of British society, including its prisons.

WIth most men fighting abroad and the women left behind filling the numerous jobs required to support the war effort, prisons had been left to fester with overcrowding being the norm and a lack of staff, including male and female officers, and high staff turnover hampering any form of operation beyond simple incarceration. The response was a plan to build five more prisons and six more borstals to ease the overcrowding over the next five years.

Prescoed had already been built by 1939, constructed by prison labourers and serving as an open borstal for the first years of its existence. It was only formally purchased by the Home Office in 1945, as it had previously been a farm, like most of the surrounding area. After this it became a detention centre in 1964 and then changed to an open youth custody centre in 1983. It became an open young offender institution in 1988, taking Category D adult males a few years later. Since 2004, it has been exclusively an open prison for adult males.

The one constant has been the word 'open' in all of Prescoed's various incarnations. In a prison setting, this implies that the prisoners are trusted to serve their sentences with minimal supervision and security and they are often not locked up In their prison cells. Prescoed's role as an open facility is likely to have been used by the Home Office to ease overcrowding after the war, by moving prisoners on who were ready for work or training to the camp.

Sport as recreation and a form of 'purposeful activity' has been used consistently in prisons since the post-war years. Sport, including football, is very effective at engaging men in different programmes designed to improve their behaviour and the way they think or react. Football has been used to improve the culture in prisons for years, such as helping prisoners get to know their surroundings, their fellow inmates and the prison officers. Reports from the Prison Department in the 1960s show a progressive attitude where teams from the surrounding areas would come into the prison to play competitive fixtures in sports such as football, basketball, rugby, cricket and squash.[3] Interestingly, the focus was less on results; perhaps it was at this moment that the first steps towards sport for rehabilitation purposes were being taken. The prisons were keen to see what 'standards of skill' were on offer by their players, as well as how the prisoners' 'sportsmanship' was affected by these competitions. These activities were clearly quite novel and unique as it was reported that interest in them amongst the prisoners was always piqued by these fixtures.

The liberal attitudes of the 1960s allowed these activities to flourish, with one report even recommending the addition of swimming pools at certain prisons, so that prisoners could take Royal Life Saving Society awards. This was a time when prison sport included open camping and inter-county weightlifting. In fact, a team of prisoners from Morton Hall competed in several annual national orienteering championships and were even placed in the top ten teams in the UK.

Football was also a beneficiary of the liberal policies and prisoner teams from Yorkshire and the Midlands by the late 1960s were competing against outside teams in local leagues. Wakefield who had been competing in their local league since the late fifties were held up at this time for celebration, having finished in the top six each season. Prisoner footballers at this time were being encouraged to take both their coaching badges and their refereeing qualifications, alongside prison staff. Even at this stage it was recognised that there was an important role for the governing bodies of sport to give both their time and support to prison staff for this to happen. Also, the role of physical education, sport and recreation was seen as crucial in developing effective relationships with the surrounding community. Professionally too, things were changing with the increase in recruitment of PEOs seeing a high number of applicants by the mid-seventies, far more than there were places available, including the first female PEOs being employed by 1976. This recruitment saw the beginnings of the provision of physical activity programmes for female prisoners as well as men.

This continues up to the present day. A recent government review of sport in all aspects of criminal justice highlighted how engaging in sports activities as part of resettlement can help reduce reoffending to as little as 6%, when the national average for reoffending in the first year after release is currently 29%.[4] The review suggested all prisons should have a strategy for developing sport, including using it as a tool for educational development, as a way of raising awareness of healthy living, and as a means of helping to improve behaviour and anger management. It also recommended developing links with local communities, as Prescoed's football team does when playing in an outside league.

Although all six prisons in Wales engage in sport, physical education and recreation, only Prescoed currently has the ability to field a football team playing in a local league, because it is Wales's only open prison. Annual prison inspection reports, which analyse and monitor all aspects of prison life, mention the presence of football at Prescoed only infrequently. Local press have no knowledge of the team or its results and you cannot simply turn up unannounced to a prison to watch a game or chat to the players. There is as much information as one would imagine on the league website: fixtures, league tables and scores only. Instead, one has to explore the world of Fanzines for any detailed information on the team's early days.

The first thing to note about Prescoed is that their performances each season are remarkable, but remarkable by design. However the design is not theirs as the club are forced to play by the FAW in the basement of Welsh football, in the Gwent Central League Division Two. Whilst accepting this decision, the club and the league are frustrated that Prescoed cannot progress from the bottom division. They cannot be promoted. The official reason given is that the team can only play in Division 2 because it is technically outside the FAW pyramid. If the division were included in the pyramid structure then, theoretically, Prescoed *could* progress upwards through the various Welsh leagues all the way to the top: the Welsh Premier League. This carries with it potential qualification for European tournaments such as the Champions League or Europa League – quite a thought for the FAW and HMPPS administrators! So they are doomed, like a footballing Sisyphus pushing a giant football up to the top of the division each year, only for it to roll back down and start over again the following season.

Football is a big deal in prison. It's used to keep people healthy through weekly social games. There are also plenty of supervised mini-tournaments, where wing goes up against wing on the prison Astro, with plenty of spectators cheering on their boys. Football is part of the culture of prisons and it has been for years. Nowhere is this truer than in Prescoed.

The Prescoed team is thought to have first entered the Gwent Central League in the late 90s and has remained a member ever since. Recollections from players of other clubs from that time refer to the immaculate pitch as being one of the best they'd played on. At that time, permanent ground staff worked with prisoners on work placement to maintain the pitches and keep them in tiptop condition. The uniqueness of the occasion (playing against serving prisoners) is still remembered fondly almost twenty years on, when it was include in a *Memories* section in Welsh Football, the grassroots fanzine for the footballing nation.[5] The article noted the uniqueness of the occasion, clearly not lost despite the passage of time.

Throughout their history, Prescoed have frequently come top in the *Best of Wales* charts compiled annually by Welsh Football. They have won their division ten out of the last fifteen seasons, regularly setting records in the process. Often they score the most goals in a season in Wales, resulting in the highest goal per game ratio and the biggest goal difference. They frequently go a full season either undefeated or winning all their games, showing they know how to both attack and defend on the pitch. The culmination of their stellar performances came in the 2018/19 season when they won all twenty games played to win the league comfortably, conceding just seventeen goals but scoring a Welsh football record of two hundred and sixty-four goals! An average of over thirteen goals per game.

Each team they come up against are well aware of this daunting reputation, adding pressure on both the visitors and the players who have to uphold it. Sometimes it feels like the opposition is playing for the runners up spot and that despite rarely winning against Prescoed it is the results against all the other teams that are the ones that matter in the fight for promotion. Teams finishing second or third behind Prescoed get promoted instead.

Welcome to Prescoed

Much like the experience of actually going to prison, the drive to HMP Prescoed should not be taken lightly. Being transported there from literally anywhere in England or Wales by a British Prisoner Transport Vehicle, with its blacked out windows, in an individual mobile cell just about big enough for you to sit up straight, must mean you are thrown all over the place, for the journey takes you through country lanes far away from the smooth A roads. You can't lean forward or stretch out like you would in a car; it must feel very claustrophobic. One can only imagine the relief when you reach your destination. That's because there are only two single track roads you can take to get there either from the south or the north. Either way, if you meet another car, tractor or one of the numerous blue minibuses taking men to their place of work from the prison, one of you will be reversing for a quite a while before the other can pass. The two-metre high hedgerows are only interrupted by the entrances to farms that pepper the four-mile journey from either direction. Add heavy winter rain, flooded roads, errant escaped sheep, dozens of potholes, occasional road kill, hairpin bends, blind corners and a gradient that will test the pulling power of the lowest gears, it should not be a surprise that some people will only accept lifts there rather than volunteering to drive themselves. At least, they won't volunteer twice.

Prescoed greets its visitors not with ten-metre high steel doors, airlock style security or intrusive searches of your entire person like that in a closed prison. Instead, a single automatic traffic barrier controlled by genial security staff is the sole arbiter of who gets in and who gets out. This simple, juddering aluminium white pole is the first clue that things in Prescoed are done differently. It is a resettlement prison, a Category D open jail where the men inside are prepared for release and life back in their communities at the end of their prison sentences. Not everyone comes to a prison like Prescoed but the ones who arrive usually have about two years remaining before they are released.

The traffic barrier isn't a deterrent to escape of course. You walk around it once your visitor security checks have been passed. Instead, it simply controls the flow of vehicles coming in and out, such as staff or delivery vehicles, so that there are checks as to who's on camp at any one time.

For the prisoners it is a physical representation of the two words heard a lot when you talk to anyone about the regime at Prescoed. Those words are *responsibility* and *trust*. As a prisoner, you are expected to take *responsibility* for yourself and most importantly you are *trusted* not to escape. All prisoners will have been risk assessed continually throughout their prison sentence to determine whether they present a risk of absconding. The traffic barrier is the last test of the old ways in closed conditions.

Some men, especially those who have done a long prison sentence, can have a sense of Cat D being a kind of utopian promised land. An open facility you can walk about freely even in the evening, where you are not confined to your cell or wing for up to twenty-two hours a day. A place you can get a job, earn a wage, go on town visits, visit your family for up to five days. But if you coming off the back of a long prison sentence you will have spent the last few years following in an incredibly regimented and structured regime where, no matter how you felt about it, whether good, bad or indifferent, you will have had no choice but to follow it. That is because there will have been several hundred other men doing exactly the same every single day, so what works for one works for all. You are told when to get up, when to eat, when to go to education, when to go to work, when to go to your cell, when it's lights out and so and so on, day after day, seven days a week, month after month, year after year. Your only freedom is really what you do in your cell and when you use its toilet. And even this may be dictated to you by your cell-mate!

Prescoed is the antithesis of life in a closed prison. Put simply and with the expected restrictions on the type of behaviour not tolerated in any prison, if you want something to happen, it is your responsibility. Want to work and earn money for when you get out of prison? Want to train and get a qualification? Want to play football? Want to apply for town leave? These all happen only if you seize the opportunities given to you by your new home for the next two years. Want to stay in bed all day and avoid the world? Then that's your responsibility too.

Interestingly, both prisoners and visitors sometimes struggle with the change and transition to the very open nature of Prescoed's prison life. The sound of a closed prison is the sound of the jangle of keys of a prison officer, opening and closing countless huge, iron doors on a journey of even just a few metres. Alarms going off at all times for all reasons. The loud, brash unselfconscious banter of men and teenagers calling out to each other across balconies and walkways. The dull droning white noise of an industrial facility incarcerating several hundred men in a few hundred square metres.

The sound of Prescoed is the absence of such sounds. Prescoed is the sound of the one hundred and fifty foot pine trees swaying in the Welsh south easterly breeze. The cawing of jackdaws that live in their branches. The noise of airbrakes being applied by the occasional delivery truck bringing supplies to the prison.

The reason for the contrast is because nearly all the two hundred and thirty men at Prescoed are engaged in education courses or work both on and off the prison site in all kinds of different jobs. The biggest employer of prison labour is its own Cilwrgi Farm, a five minute, blue minibus drive away to the south. Across the farm's four hundred and twenty acre estate there are over a hundred cows that need milking twice a day to supply some well-known supermarket yoghurt brands. Plus, there are one hundred and sixty acres of woodland with its own sawmill. The rest of the men are either working in the prison kitchens, or as cleaners, in the recycling plant, or as support workers in more specialised units like induction, where those who have just arrived are settled in to prison life. It can be a pretty quiet place except for when gym or football is involved. That's when Prescoed comes alive.

Like all male prisons, the gym is a focal point of activity. Prescoed's is not hard to find. It is in the middle of the prison and advertises its opening hours by the loud hardcore house music pumping out from the stereo within. A small standalone building with functional windows looking down across the site's green tapestry of clipped lawns, flowerbeds and meandering footpaths, it is just like most of the buildings at Prescoed. But as you approach the door, walk past the windows and look inside, you see, hear and smell the experience of men who live for working out.

The bikes and treadmills, although well used, are easier to get on than the free heavy weights, which are the most prized possession there. Pairs of men arrive as soon as the gym opens and their training session begins. Steel barbells bow under one hundred and fifty kilogram weights as they are pressed and forced upwards by chests and arms, bursting with effort and intensity. Lean, sweating, triangular shaped men with body fat percentages in single figures channelling every lock up, every judge's decision, every removal of liberty into each repetition. Teeth constantly gritted with the exertion; there's no small talk here, no banter. A loud "Urgh!" signals the final rep of a lift, followed by the thump of the huge weights dropping to the floor in triumph, vibrating the TV on the wall subtitling bland daytime TV shows, discussing subjects of little interest to the men in the prison.

This gym is therapy. Each man's impressive, gym-chiselled stature acting as both a physical and mental defensive shield to the world. When they are spent physically, they rest mentally. Then it's time to recover and sleep, ready to train all over again, tomorrow, day after day, seven days a week, month after month, year after year.

Football also provides therapy at Prescoed, but a less testosterone-fuelled or overtly macho version as that up on the hill. Tuesday afternoon is training, and half an hour before any sign of a PEO to open up the changing rooms and blow up the footballs, men are congregating and exchanging stories. They are excited, teasing and scoring points off one another, reminding each other how well they played last time and how badly the others fared. The noise levels rise as more arrive and the pecking order emerges. It's the senior players who are teased more than the new arrivals. Their status as longer serving prisoners, comfortable in their surroundings, presenting a sense of authority ripe for taking down a peg or two. Except they've got more than enough answers and the verbal sparring adds to the noise.

There are always new players who have just arrived that week. Together, but separate from the pack, unless they know some of the players from prior stints in other Welsh jails. Then they are greeted warmly like all friends and are immediately 'in', especially if they've got form – in other words if they are known to be good players. For those just shipped in who are unknown, the experience of playing football on a grass pitch, rather than on a concrete five-a-side pitch in a closed prison, is just one of a number of new experiences Prescoed presents. It's these men who stay quiet, eyes keenly watching and taking everything in. Every prisoner has been there before, even if they are on their fifth prison sentence now. The questions are the same: "What's your name? Where you from? Where you been?" intended to create a sense of connection with a new player. There's honour amongst prisoners created by an automatic bond conferred by the label 'prisoner' and locked up by the state with common challenges ahead today, and in the future.

The Officer arrives to open up the changing rooms, one of four whose shifts rotate at any one time. The waiting players tease him every week that he's late (they aren't) and you understand that whatever time the changing rooms were opened, it wouldn't ever be early enough. The teasing goes back and forth just as it does with the senior players and you realise that this is different. Prison Officers are not normally spoken to like this.

Officially, the role of sport in prison plays a part as one of the seven Reducing Reoffending Pathways in Wales.[6] These 'pathways' are in place to support individuals out of previous offending behaviour and provide the focus for the combined efforts of both criminal justice and other agencies to support offenders with the best opportunities to reform. All the pathways are linked, as you would imagine. An example would be the Accommodation pathway, which is closely linked to Finance, Benefit, Debt and Advice, meaning a place to live is dependent on your housing benefit being received. Sport fits into the Health pathway of the strategy, but closer examination shows that this is mainly concerned with mental health and substance misuse.

Staff at Prescoed have seen first-hand how sport and particularly football has helped prisoners. "Football is here to reconnect the men with their families and the community on the pitch. It opens up the world to them after release. It challenges the attitudes, thinking and behaviour of even hardened criminals," explained Governor West, who has been in the prison service since 1996. "It's a bit of normality for the men here. We use football as engagement. That way we can build relationships, to help them work together as a team. That's shown by the behaviour here; it's always been good. Most of the trouble comes from the visiting teams. Even the refs like coming here."

In previous years, staff have played alongside prisoners in the team, something which until this season hadn't happened that much. But changes in staff have brought new ways of working for the prison. Prescoed comes under the joint management of a Governor with responsibility for HMP Usk and Cilwrgi Farm, and a staff team has been formed to play other prisons, as well as against the prisoner team. This game, in fact, was watched by a combination of staff and prisoners mixing and mingling like any other park football match on a Saturday. Although the game was won by the staff team, the significance of the event was marked by the prison's governor who commissioned a plaque to commemorate the match and committed to making it an annual event, even giving the players a small increase in their day's pay as recognition. That was because nearly all the prisoners who played took time off their work so they could play in the game. They were not going to miss the opportunity to go up against the staff!

A prisoner versus staff match isn't the only notable game of football to happen at Prescoed. Back in the 1998/99 season, Bobby Gould (the former Wales Manager) regularly brought the Wales squad for training sessions to the prison as part of their preparations for the 2000 European Championships. This was an arrangement set up by the Wales team's Travel Agent who was also a former Prescoed resident! At the time the Wales players stayed in the nearby Cwrt Bleddyn Hotel, Usk and were looking for a training base close to their accommodation. The utilisation of the facilities at Prescoed, had additional advantages. The security of the prison meant that kit and equipment could be left there overnight without fear of it going missing. Also the kit men were able to utilise the prison laundry staff to wash and dry the training kit in readiness for the following day's training session. The cost of this arrangement? The 'currency' of a signed shirt or ball!

On one occasion, when the team were running through set pieces and patterns of play, Neville Southall (the Wales goalkeeper at the time) wanted to add some realism to the set-up instead of using plastic mannequins, which simply stick in the ground and don't move. So Southall asked the prison guards if he could 'borrow' a couple of inmates to play up front, to drag the defenders around the pitch a bit and put them under some pressure. Three or four inmates were chosen and are said to have performed their roles very ably, but sadly not well enough to gain full selection for the starting line-up! Soon after this period, the Wales team changed hotels and consequently never returned to either Cwrt Bleddyn or HMP Prescoed again.[7]

Although Prescoed's two pitches are far better than most others belonging to their Gwent Central League compatriots, back then, Prescoed had their own ground staff with prison labour to help create a lush, flat and well-preserved playing service. Added to the secure nature of its secluded location, it made an ideal 'secret' training camp. Doncaster Rovers also used it in preparation for their victory over Bristol Rovers in the Johnstone's Paint Trophy in 2006 at the (former) Millennium Stadium.

Even twenty years on, the Wales squad's visit is still etched in the memory of the staff who were there. "Bobby Gould took a training session here. We usually just did skills and drills but this was a real eye-opener. I remember we got to play against some of the Welsh squad and although I'm fit I was chasing shadows with the likes of Coleman and Pembridge on there. We couldn't get near them," remembered Governor West, whose prison-hardened exterior dissolves when he talks about his memories of football at Prescoed. A programme from the Wales versus Denmark game in 1999 contains a photo of Bobby Gould and Gary Speed presenting him with a signed Wales shirt. It still sits, pride of place, in his modest office to this day.

The squad back then contained players who are still household names today: Speed, Hartson, Saunders, Bellamy, Hughes and Southall, for example. But the experience at Prescoed is remembered less favourably by the current manager who also played there, Ryan Giggs: "Prisons? I don't want that for my players. One of my frustrations during my Wales playing days was training on parks and bogs".[8] The contrast between the current state of the art training facilities most national teams enjoy, including Wales, and what was offered at Prescoed reflects the changing nature of elite football since the advent of the Premier League. There are programmes looking to connect football clubs with their communities, including prisons, often through the work of their charitable foundations, such as Cardiff City and Newport County. However, it would be unlikely to see a national team visiting and training in a prison again, organised by their governing football association, as it currently stands.

Instead, the use of football in any prison and especially at Prescoed comes down to the effect the experience has on the individuals. Whether it is someone coming to training on Tuesday afternoons, or those selected for the match on a Saturday, the opportunity is unique. Prisoners transferring to Prescoed know about the football team, but their knowledge is patchy, made up of half-heard stories and exaggerations. People think they are just there to kick a ball, but through the deliberate actions of the prison staff overseeing the activities and also through a process of osmosis, as new players are integrated into the sport, there is clearly a transformative aspect to Prescoed's football experience.

Once changed into their kit, everyone together makes the hundred and fifty metre walk through the woods to the pitch. The trees are pine and grow quickly, like many similar woods and forests across Britain. This one was planted after the First World War to provide a reserve of timber, since the country had lost so many oaks and other slow-growing trees as a consequence of the war. They were likely planted just before the prison was built, when it was originally an open borstal designed to reform young people through a combination of work, education and recreation, principles that may still be seen in the way that the prison today assists its adult population.

The walk takes longer than anticipated, as the precarious earthen path takes you through a steep up-and-down trajectory as you cross over Dowlais Brook; plus it is bare and dark at ground level. Pine trees are notoriously acidic, so not much else grows where they thrive. Instead, the trees are packed tightly, stretching high above, competing for sunlight, so all the foliage is above bare tree trunks. Badger sets, the nemesis of the groundsman, can be seen in the banks of the uphill sections of the walk. A tumbledown, abandoned fertilizer shed, tucked out of the way, provides a too obvious temptation for anyone scouting for a drop off point for drugs, booze or mobile phones, all banned in the prison. "There are cameras in the woods," the Prison Officer warns you the first time you walk through.

At the path's conclusion, you emerge onto the training pitch, which runs adjacent to the main pitch and is about ten metres higher. It offers an elevated, spectator's-eye view of the game, useful for tactical observations. Even on the dullest day, the effect of emerging from dark trees into daylight is visually similar to players emerging from the players' tunnel before a game at a football league ground. You arrive at a place of football and competition.

You have been transported into arguably one of the most scenic places to play football in Wales. Below you is the lush green match day pitch, with white posts, corner flags and nets all ready to receive both teams, bordered on three sides by trees. Ahead of you rises a patchwork quilt of fields containing sheep, cattle and two picturesque, chocolate box farmhouse cottages, often with a picturesque plume of smoke from a chimney disappearing into the sky. You are in the countryside, a rural idyll.

What you cannot see from the pitch is the prison. There are no walls, barriers or barbed wires. Just two teams ready for a game of football. It is this juxtaposition with a regular prison environment that provides the most significant feature of Prescoed's football culture.

Before the match you watch the players going through their paces. Small cliques of men who are familiar with each other naturally form, and within each clique the men are quick to pass the ball to each other. Others, often the new arrivals and the forwards, take turns shooting and missing at the goal, as crosses arrive from either corner. It's a practice seen before most local league games and provides instant redemption for those who connect with a volley, striking the ball into the goal past the goalkeeper. It's useful too for the new players to size up their fellow players. The misses send the ball boys scrambling into the brambles to retrieve each errant strike. The ball boys are also fellow prisoners grateful for a couple of hours to watch a game. The joking and banter that always accompany the misses provides the opportunity to know each player's name and form. The jovial atmosphere helping players relax.

To an outsider, everyone is the same. But a quick inventory of the players' football boot colours shows who is new and who isn't. Those who've been at Prescoed only a few days or weeks use the boots from the stores, prison issue Hummel football boots in all sizes and colours, as long as they are black. The more established prisoners have had their boots sent from home and their bright vivid colours are a metaphor of the extension of their desire to express their individuality and the beginnings of personal freedom that come with life in an open prison. No prison issue grey sweats and trainers for them anymore.

The opposition emerge from the trees and down to the pitch, with Prescoed's players sizing them up as much as they can. Starved of up to date information, prisoners are not permitted to use the internet. The men have no idea if a first team match is off or if the opposition team is full of ringers, for example. The arrival of their opponents stimulates an intensity in the team's preparations and the senior players gather everyone together to go through a warm up and passing drills. Paul, the most vocal of all the players, senior or junior, is the marshal. An ex-professional footballer who the others defer to with his call to action and choice of drills. They know this is his domain and follow his lead. By the time kick-off arrives everyone knows their job and their responsibility to win. There is no room for negotiation.

The final word goes to the PEO as an acknowledgement of his status as a prison officer. He urges the basics, to keep possession and play football, but also not to let the referee's decisions or the opposition's entourage get into the players' heads. Several of the men have prison convictions due to or closely related to violence. The football provides a physical but controlled release of both energy and emotion for both teams, but for Prescoed's players the stakes by design are higher. A verbal or physical response to any provocation could result in a loss of family visits or being sent back to a closed prison. Players understand that they could get more than a yellow or red card; they could get charged with an *incident.* The loss of football would be a side issue in their journey of one step forward and two steps back towards rehabilitation.

"Prison is a very selfish place and the players can struggle being in a team environment. Football can help them understand that their actions have implications," explains Mr Snape, one of the four PEOs responsible for the sport and exercise activities in the prison. "Some prisoners when they come to Cat D and its open conditions with home leave and going out to work, they forget they are still in prison."

Fellow PEO Mr Harrison explains how football can help: "It's good for anger management. The inmate on the wing has one set of rules: prison rules. But here with the football we have prison rules, the PE Department rules and the governing body's rules. So PE comes into its own that way." The rules of the department tend to be etiquette based, so whether it's looking after sports kit or putting equipment away after they've been used, non-adherence to them swiftly results in activities being cancelled. These experiences are isolated incidents and the men quickly police the situation themselves. The withdrawal of the gym for a day particularly, causes much finger pointing and upheaval. Actions or inactions especially have consequences beyond those at fault at Prescoed.

Like a lot of football on a Saturday, the presence of a referee is always greeted with a mixture of relief and enthusiasm, as it means the coach from either team will not have to officiate. Interestingly, at Prescoed, if a referee is needed it is usually the PEO who steps up, not the opposition's representative. "The refs coming up here say this is the place to come. They don't get any rubbish here and the visiting teams don't get any physical abuse here either," explains PEO Mr Davies. "A lot of the lads are in for responding badly to situations as part of their crime. They are capable of quite violent acts, but here they tend to be better behaved."

Mr Harrison agrees: "Some players develop personally so much. I've seen players who were like an empty packet of crisps before a game turn into a man by the final whistle. We help them to find self-control. One player I knew was on the end of a very bad tackle. But he got up, kept himself in check and walked away shouting 'My anger management is working, Sir!'"

"There have been some excellent players that have come through here in my time. We used to have short-term prisoners but over the last eight or nine years the prison has started to accept longer term prisoners so we are able to maintain better teams. We have the lads for one or two seasons quite often.

"We see ourselves as mentors more than anything, though we are Prison Officers not *civvies*. We've all worked on the wings. We've seen the other side to life where you are dealing with people in a non-conforming environment, where prisoners just see the black and white shirt. The PE staff are all on the same wavelength and [have] been in the job a long time. We are strong characters, you have to be. Here we offer something the prisoners want, whether it's football or the gym, so they won't bite the hand that feeds them."

The PE office is a regular haunt of some players if they are not working off camp. Men will come in for a chat under the auspices of Saturday's league game, but conversations regularly steer towards life beyond Prescoed: family, employment, going straight. PEO Mr Moore acknowledges the role they play in the prisoners' lives: "Some of the boys have a hard time at home from their partners, because they are serving a sentence too. While their boyfriend or husband or kid's dad is in here away from it all, they are the ones having to look after the kids, do the school run, pay the bills - it's hard. The men come in here and talk things through with us. I've had the biggest men, the ones you wouldn't expect, in tears right here in this office. Some of them, I've grown up in the same circumstances to them, but where I've taken one path, they've taken another. We teach them life-skills, how to not react, how to walk away, how to cope."

To the observer, this is the heartbeat of football at Prescoed and the root of its success. Of course, the men are fitter than their non-prisoner opposition and have no distractions like shift work, childcare or going to the pub to watch a game instead. However, this only tells one side of the story. The importance of the relationships between those involved and the men who play for Prescoed FC mean that football is more than a game, more than the sum of its parts for these men.

To the opposition, Prescoed are the team to come runners-up to as they have won the Gwent Central Division Two (or its equivalent) many times. Prescoed is also a place where they know there will not be any trouble on the sideline, a view shared by the match officials.

To the senior prison hierarchy, football may be seen as an engagement tool upon which to hang rehabilitative behaviours, such as anger management and etiquette, which it does successfully. With the players and the ball boys, football may be a way to enjoy a couple of hours off camp and a way to keep fit. To the new arrivals, it is the opportunity to adapt to open conditions and meet new people. To those on long sentences, it is a bit of normality, the opportunity to reset themselves back to how things were when they were younger before they went to prison. To the PEOs, it is an opportunity to have a potentially lasting impact on those both at training and on match days. Through the mentoring-like approach, the skills learnt and honed on the pitch replicate those learnt and honed in the open prison environment.

So, for the author, it was important to do more than simply record and notate results, scorers and league positions. To try to understand what this 'greater than the sum of its parts' could be and what it could mean, it was important to ask the individuals who play week in, week out. Their stories and their experiences shape this book and, whilst acknowledging that each person is there because a crime has been committed, it was of equal importance to understand the human aspect of each person's unique journey. Football was playing a part in their preparation for release from jail. These are their stories.

Sam

The man who hasn't made a mistake, hasn't done anything.

Goalkeeper
Induction Orderly

So, a bit about me. I'm married, over twenty five years with two sons and two grandsons. I'm 47 years old now, so a bit old to be playing football! It's my first time in prison, but I'm here and there's not a lot I can do about it now.

I played football since the age of 8 but not always in goal. I trialled for a professional club at the age of fifteen or sixteen; unfortunately broke my wrist in one of the trial games and stopped playing for a while. When I broke my wrist I couldn't play in goal, so I started playing in the middle of the park and played well there. And I've been playing until I was 47 years old until I hurt my leg recently and had to pack it in.

I'm a level one rugby coach and I've done a lot of coaching with my local club because my youngest boy from the age of eight was playing rugby as well. I took him through until he was fifteen. I played at a tidy level too, local, in one of the highest leagues back home and won a few championships with the boys. I've been involved with my local club for about twenty years now, who my boys play for. I played alongside my oldest son and it was a special moment. I enjoyed it because on the day it was family affair: myself, my son in the middle of the pack, my nephew on the left hand side, my other nephew on the right hand side, and my other nephew was playing centre forward, so I was playing along with all of them. Now, my youngest boy is hoping I can play alongside the two of them, when I'm out. I haven't told my wife yet, but it's something I look forward to.

This is my first time in prison. I got done for burglary with intent. It was actually a bit of a scuffle inside a house; something had gone on earlier in the night. My youngest son found out about it; he's gone down to this guy's house. I found out my son has gone down; when I got there he had hold of my son [and] I just barged the door with my shoulder. The door got damaged and we had a scuffle inside the porch. My son broke it up and me and my son both got done for burglary with intent because he said that once we got inside the house, we pulled him out of bed, stamped all over him and kicked him. A day before it went to court I admitted to everything. So that they would drop the charges against my son. Any father would have pleaded guilty so as not to have their son having anything, you know. First offence. And they put me in jail.

Hopefully, I get out in a couple of months, which they say I probably will. It's been hard. We lost our daughter twenty years ago, she passed away, so my wife really struggles. I tried to put that over to the judge. Haven't been in trouble before, but they weren't having any of it because I pleaded guilty to stop my son having anything. A lot of people just shake their heads; they can't understand why I'm in here, but here I am and I've just got to get on with it.

A lot of people have said that I don't seem like a normal prisoner. But it's a part of my life now that I've got to get on with. Hopefully, I get my first Town Leave and then I'm home for five days. I've got sit before the board, but it's more or less a formality really, but I've got to go back and start rebuilding my life.

Before here I was in S------ from the day before my birthday until August when I got moved straight to the enhanced wing, moved straight to the library doing a good job. Within two weeks I was D Cat and they asked me to come up here. Well, they told me I was coming up here, but the library put me on hold because I was doing a good job but I was happy to stay there. They tried again a month later, and I said, "Look, I'm happy to stay here". But then the library put me on hold and they thought third time lucky: you're going to Prescoed. I didn't want to go. As you can imagine, first time in prison, rabbit in the headlights, after a couple of weeks, I just wanted to get in there. S------ was closer to my house and my wife doesn't drive. But looking back it was the best thing because I didn't see my grandson. When he came up here, its four hours in a car isn't it? He thinks I'm working away and come home late, so that's the plus side.

When I got here then, within a few weeks, I got a job in the library and then I got offered the induction job, which I've done for a while and now they've made me a key worker. In fact, I'm here, I'm sorry I didn't come the first time. Out of a bad situation, this is the best it's going to get. In fact, when I came into prison, I lost four kilograms from the stress.

Going to the gym in prison really helped, but the only sport they had there was 5-a-side football on a small Astroturf and I didn't really fancy doing that. So I really only did the gym, and we used to play bowls on a mat every Friday because I used to play bowls on the outside as well. So I played and I'd have a game against G Wing. Undefeated as well, which is a good thing. That's the only sport I played for a while.

I heard about the football at Prescoed before I came here. There was a guy that used to play with us; he was up here with us last year. A really good football player, youngster, but in and out of jail he was. When I first played properly with him he had my number. I used to wear number sixteen because I thought I was Roy Keane! But he wore number sixteen and when he left he brought the shirt with him. He was supposed to hand it in! I've known him since he was a kid and he said he'd played at Prescoed and had banged the goals in and things, but I didn't think I'd get involved. My wife said "Oh, you can't play, you can't play!" but I love my sport. I was always going to get involved when I came here even if it's just fetching the water, getting the ball or running the line. It's a good thing that's happened to me here. As well as my induction job, it's one of the positives that comes out of me being in prison I think.

It's been great playing here. What it does, like what I said to the wife, is it breaks the weekend up. You look forward to it on a Saturday. When I was just helping out, no matter what the weather, I was going over anyway. A pair of boots and socks over your trousers and away you go. In fact, the involvement and the camaraderie is what makes it. Before you go to the football, when I [was] first here, I didn't know anyone. The four guys from who I came to Prescoed with, they didn't play football. Then Paul got involved and I knew him too, plus Alan when he came here. When they got involved it was great. It was that chance of looking forward to something on the weekend: football on a Saturday, visit on a Sunday. Like when you're back home, you can't wait for the weekend to come with the football, watching my kids play. So when the weekend comes that's what it is all about. It's good, you know?

We're a real team too. You can see at certain times when there is a bit of an argument or the opposition puts a good ball through. We all know what each other can do and how we play, so if anyone doesn't do it, sometimes they get frustrated. Sometimes it's their own fault and sometimes it's another boy's fault. But if we score a goal then we settle down and start playing football. I think, when there's confidence, it helps you work as a team. For me, there's also some positivity there to help you do your sentence.

When I play, you see the boys get changed within five minutes and are waiting for the other team to turn up every week. Then it's, "Come on, let's get over there!" You get to know the guys. It's that team element. Nobody knew my name within the first couple of weeks when I was helping out, doing the water or first aid, but now everyone knows me. It really takes you away for two hours on a Saturday and breaks the whole weekend up.

Where we play, you can't see the prison, so you could be playing anywhere. In your mind you are off camp, whenever you go over. When I first went over to the football pitch, it's like a nature walk to get there through all the trees and it just takes you away from everything, all your frustrations; if you've got frustrations or anxieties, it just gets switched off. In the summer, it was beautiful over there. The pitch was like a bowling green. In fact, even when we played in the mud, it was great.

When I came here, I said to the staff "I've been around football all my life, I've coached, played and I'm first aid trained. Can I help out?" So they put my name down and, the first thing I did, whether it's a natural thing as one of the older ones or because I wasn't playing, I filled the water-bottles up and checked the first aid bag. I forgot where I was for a minute. It reminded me of life before prison. I used to go up the park just watching a game. The wife might come with me when I'm out walking the dog. Chances are when I go up there I end up running the line and then she's left walking the dog on her own! It's that thing, I've got to get involved.

I remember once when the wife and I were decorating and we [were] scraping the wallpaper off in the living room. The first team are playing, my old club. There was a knock on the door: "Can you come and help us out? The keeper can't make it. He's stuck at work!" I'm up a ladder at this point and the wife goes "you can't go!" But I said

"Luv, I gotta go!" I went down, played football and came back home to finish the decorating. We didn't speak for about 3 days! She knows how important sport is to me.

Here it was the same. I got involved, filling the water-bottles and helping out. Then the keeper left and at first Paul went in goals, but he was too good to go in and he needed to play out. So I said, "I used to go in goals", so I went training and that's where I ended up, playing in goals again. Whenever you're an ex-keeper you tend to be asked to go in goals. "Oh we haven't got a keeper today, can you go in then?"

Football has made a bit of difference to me and some of the other boys in here. When they first come in they can be like a rabbit in headlights, just like I was too. Where I work in induction I'll start talking about football and normal things; sort of come in that way. As an older guy, it's helped me be accepted.

The youngsters, some of them here, they can walk into a room and people know them straight away. Because I'm quieter, it took me a couple of weeks to speak to the guys and things like that. There was a little bit of a clique when I first come in, but then one of the guys left and things settled down. Then Paul started playing who I knew from my previous prison and he's a big voice on the team which gives you confidence. Then I got to know the younger lads like Jermaine after a couple of weeks and he'd say, "Alright Sammy?" when he saw me and things like that. When you're a quiet person like myself, knowing that they know your name is a hell of a boost in here. It gives you confidence not only at football, but when you're coming away from the football to do a job in the prison. Plus it also helps you with your time here, I think. The positivity I get, even when I'm not playing, because the guys know me now, I'm there every week on the line. It's that confidence.

Whoever comes in now through Inductions, the first thing I say to them is "Do you play football? Any shape on you? Training is on Tuesday and we're in the league, so we play Saturdays." It's that motivation you need as a quiet guy to take that step forward. Whether you're a tidy player or not they won't exclude you at training. You can still go over whether you make the side or not. I say to all the boys to come over and be a ball boy. Some aren't interested so I explain that you are surrounded by trees and it feels like you could be anywhere in Wales, because it's two hours off the camp really.

In football, there's positivity in the changing room and on the pitch which you can definitely feel. It's very similar to when I take the boys on induction and we take them on a five minute bus ride to the farm. Some of them aren't happy and say, "I'm not going to a farm!" but then you go up there and you feel like you're off camp. Even if they don't want to work there, they're glad they came. It's the same when you're doing the football. I tell them "You go training on a Tuesday, it's a nature walk over, play for an hour, then come back. On Saturdays it's for two hours." I tell them to do it, whether their standard is good or not. I know they limit the amount of people, but I think it's great.

Some of the senior players tend to look out for the younger ones too because it's hard to give criticism either if you are playing or you are on the line. Like when one of the boys missed a penalty, Daniel straight away tapped him on the head and said "Come on, you're alright. On you go again." Specifically for the younger ones it's a big thing. And they do, they get up and go again. It comes from their knowledge and experience outside prison before they came in and were playing football. I did coach quite young, but I was also playing as well.

For me, the man who hasn't made a mistake hasn't done anything. We've all made mistakes, missed penalties, made a bad ball. But you put your hand up and say "Come on then. Call me everything under the sun". Then they tap me on the head as a joke and then we'll go on. It's just that, its banter. It's the same here. If they're having a laugh and a joke or taking the mick out of one their shots. Or asking "Did you see me score that goal?" I think that's camaraderie and it's all part of the team.

Same with the staff like Mr Moore, he lets the boys sort things out themselves first then gets involved later. Mr Williams, Mr Harris and Mr Snape, they're all good because they are quite sport minded and aren't thought of as prison officers when they're there. There might be a different element if the staff were younger but when they're over there they're a coach and a ref and that's a big thing. There's a lot of banter, but when they tell us to listen up we do.

Prison is like a conveyor belt and the nucleus of the side is going to be together one season. Daniel came in a couple of games in, Paul was a couple of games in. I was involved from the first game, as a water boy or as a ball boy, but more or less here every game.

Of all the activities that I do here, football is the most important to me. I maybe can't train every week because I have to do inductions sometimes, but that's my job on camp. For me it's Saturday football; Sunday's family. Tuesday is training, then you're looking forward to Saturday again. That seven days just flies by. When you look at it then you've played four games and that's a month of your sentence gone.

Football's had a good effect on me, but I'm currently injured and I'm putting on weight! I was laid up for three weeks. I wasn't allowed to do any Inductions. Although I was walking about when I wasn't supposed to and getting bollocked every time I left my bed! What I found was that time dragged because I had nothing to focus on. I couldn't work; I couldn't play. Look, I'm forty-seven so maybe I shouldn't have been playing anyway, but then when you've always played and then you can't, it's like dropping a fiver and finding a five pence piece. It was a kick in the balls, a kick in the guts.

So as soon as I had the ok to go back on the wing, I was told I can't play, because if I have it again, I'll have a blood clot. The boys didn't understand and they said, "Do you want to play Saturday?" But I had tell them I'm finished. If the wife would never find out then I'd maybe think about playing but it's not worth it, because she would find out! But then even the Prison Officers said they wouldn't let me play, because they were sick of doing inductions without me!

I've seen football have a hell of a positive impact on other players too. One of the boys who came in, he was a youngster but he was lucky enough to come in with two guys who knew he played football and they told me about him in Induction. So we got him involved, on the bench at first, but he came on and played well. He struggled with literacy and I helped him get involved with the football, so he comes down my room and asks for help with this and that with his writing. For a youngster coming in here it's difficult. Like me, this is his first time inside.

On the outside, these boys would have probably come through a club as a youth, then into the seniors, but in here you come into an alien environment. He knows the boys now, but he didn't at first. When Saturday comes it's another week off his sentence. He hasn't got a huge amount of time to do, but you can see he's come out of his shell a bit. Not so much rabbit in the headlights, because he's a youngster. Not cocky, but he thought he was quite hard. But I think he was quiet; when I met him in inductions, I was pleased I could help him. As a father figure you're quite proud to see that he's going to training and he's enjoying the football. You can see the guys speak to him, even if he's off to the side of things. He's got skill with the ball and he's quite quick, so I think, for next year, I don't know where he'll be at the end of the season but he'll be fine, I can tell. It's given him confidence to think, "I'm ok here, the surroundings are alright and it's a pretty place when the sun shines". He comes off camp twice a week for training and football on Saturday. It's good to see.

Football helps the boys inside here. In fact nobody does much wrong here because you can't. But for me, you've got the chance to relieve a lot of tension through the football, even if it's just booting the ball up in the air in training and having a laugh. So long as you're laughing you're not crying and laughter is the best medicine. I know I keep coming back to it but it's that camaraderie that when Saturday comes let's get out there, have a laugh, have a joke, take the piss out of each other on the way down, and then we're ready to play, heads on. When we win the game, have a laugh and a joke afterwards. That's real positivity.

Tom

All your freedom is taken away. But football, they can't really take that away from you.

Defender

I'm twenty-five and I come from the West Country. Before coming to jail I was an electrical engineer. I was involved in a car accident where someone lost their life so that's why I'm here now. Whilst in jail I want to do everything I can to better myself for future release. I've got a daughter, partner, quite a close-knit family. It was quite a shock coming to a prison, but I'm trying to make the best of the current situation.

I used to play football from when I was about six or seven, all the way up through the ages. Then I started playing adult football with a good group of lads and I enjoyed that. When I was eighteen, I took my level one FA football coaching badge for about six or seven months. I [was] coaching the local under sixes on a Saturday morning, which was a good laugh. I played to quite a decent standard. I used to play Sunday football, five-a-side. Any sort of football, I played, really. It was good exercise and I enjoyed the social side of things.

When I was in HMP P------- for twenty-one months they had a football academy in there, which was every morning. It was probably fifteen lads run by one of the PE instructors. It was a good laugh, a bit different to going to work. It was good experience; we used to play outside teams as well. We played Hackney Wick where all the ex-prisoners come in. They were run by an ex-prisoner, which was an experience. He told us some of their stories. Their manager told us how he had changed himself while he was in jail, to then go out and run his own football team. That meant a lot. We were beating them two nil for about thirty-five minutes, then after that everyone's legs went and we lost five two. For forty minutes we gave a good game. They started arguing and had a bit of a moan when they thought they might get beaten by a prisoner team!

We had a couple more games around December, so it was good to have something to focus on around Christmas and get your head out of jail for a day really. I was in a YOI and it gives you that few hours out of jail and takes your mind of things. A bit of a respite, something to focus on rather than just the day-to-day of being in jail. When you're with your mates playing football, it's a helpful experience really.

I've been at Prescoed for nine weeks now. As soon as I got here, I was speaking to a couple of the boys and they said there was a football team. So I thought that's a good thing to do and they play in a league every Saturday. I knew I wanted to get involved in that. I like my sport and I'd like to go back to playing football again when I get out. So, anything I can do while in here is going to be a good thing for me. Before I came here

I'd heard a few people say that they knew people who have come here and said there was a team, but until you get here you just don't know.

All they said was there was a football team. I didn't realise it was a week in, week out league. So, when I arrived, I thought that was a good thing because it guaranteed me playing every week. But then I didn't realise how good they were. They've won quite a few games and scored a lot of goals. That was better than playing in my old prison, losing all the time!

Football in jail helps. You get to meet a different group of lads, get to hear different lads' stories. It's a good way of meeting people, socialising, a good form of exercising and breaks your time up in jail. When you're out there playing football, it takes your mind off things. Football is like a bit of normality when all your freedom is taken away. But football, they can't really take that away from you. When you're playing football, it's good, you know. It sort of releases your endorphins, makes you feel good about yourself. So it's… what's the word? It improves your mental health.

It's given me focus again. When you play every week you've got that focus. You want to train, you want to be out there playing. With the weather it's not great at the minute, but it's something to focus your time and energy on rather than worrying about being here.

I think it's helped a lot, because when you get here you don't really know anyone and sometimes it can be hard to get to know people, talk to people. But with football, that's taken away because you all have the same focus. It gives you the chance to talk to people, make a few friends and make your time go a bit easier. It's just that little few hours, takes your mind off things. Nothing else matters when you're playing football.

In closed conditions, it's a bit different; there's not a lot of opportunities for people to do these extra activities. With football it's a privilege, not a right, so it does help people. If you don't behave, they stop you from playing, and if you are a nuisance, they don't want you in the team. It gives you extra incentives to behave and get on with things rather than causing problems because then you would miss out. Other people would benefit from being able to play instead of you.

While I've been here, I've not seen any incidents of lads misbehaving, really. It's good for that. When you're playing you can release any stress you have, any problems you can take out on the pitch, rather than taking it back to the wings and getting yourself in trouble.

I've seen a difference between people who don't play and people in closed conditions, definitely. The people who weren't involved were jealous in a way that they weren't being picked because of their behaviour [as] opposed to those who did behave and were being picked. It provided an incentive for them to behave, especially a few of the troublemakers who wanted to be involved. So, they behaved and didn't like it when they weren't.

Besides football, I'm also working up here in the forestry, which is not a bad job. I enjoy practical things like being outside, chopping down trees, processing them, and then when the sawmill is working, cutting them down, planking. It's hard work, which I enjoy. I'm also doing a level three Open University course in Electrical Theory. I'm trying to get some funding to do a part-time college course. Plus, I go to the gym to keep fit; that's about it really.

But football has always been important me, through all my life. It's the one thing that's stayed the same through all my different ages. In fact, it means something different to me now you're in here. That's the difference. It's one of the one things you can sort of decide to do or not to do, like you would on the outside. You've got that freedom to do what you want, and obviously whilst you're in here you can't do other things, so it's nice to be able to play. It's one of the few things you've got that's a personal choice.

Football can teach you lessons. You've got to adhere to rules. It teaches you social skills, teaches you right and wrong. It gives you a good focus really. In here it just gives you that little bit of respite that can mean a lot to some people, especially me.
If it wasn't here you would almost lose a bit of your focus and drive, because there isn't that extra thing to do. When you start the week on a Monday, you think, "Oh, I've got football on Saturday", and then on Saturday, you think, "Oh, I've got football again next Saturday". So you've got something to work towards for that week. You can work out how much time you've got left. You can think I've got X amount of games until I'm out and you can tick it down that way. So you've got ten games in a season I'll think, "I've got twenty games of football left and then I'm home".

I'm hoping to go back to the team that I was playing with before, or there's a few sort of local teams that I know that I can go and play for too. Most of my good mates are still playing for them and when they come and visit me, they let me know how they are getting on. I know a couple of the managers, so I always ask how they are getting on. My dad goes and watches now and again. To see how they're getting on, he used to play for them thirty, forty years ago. My dad's looking forward to seeing me play again when I get out. He's into his sport and he's been my football manager ever since I started playing really.

With some of the younger players, it's a bit like a father and son relationship with the staff because they're older. When you're in prison there's not many people you can look up to, a role model in a way, so the PE staff take that responsibility, because there's no one else that can do that.

Without any football here, I think it would have made the time drag a bit more; it would have felt longer, because you haven't got that focus for Saturday afternoons. It takes a lot of stress away and makes people feel better about themselves. Give them a bit of confidence that when they get out, they don't need to reoffend; they can change their lives around. They don't need to come back to this environment.

I don't want to be in this sort of situation again. Once I'm out I want to stay out; I don't want to come back. Anything I can do to change that I'm all for really. That's all of us in the football team. It's a good group of lads. We have the same mentality.

Bailey

We're a football team not a prisoner team, so we've got additional hidden responsibilities.

Defender

So, I'm thirty-seven now and my main sports for the last fifteen years have been golf and football. Prior to that I played a lot of rugby but unfortunately injury forced me to give that a miss. Before that I was playing up until two to three years before I came to Prescoed. The birth of my daughter put that on the back burner. I've been at Prescoed [for] four months and before that I spent ten months in C----- I've been playing football since I've been here.

Before I started playing football, it was mainly gym, taking the dog for a walk, going for a run, that sort of thing. Sport in prison, like [at] HMP C------ where I was before, they do a lot of five-a-side twice a week, on the 3G pitch and then a few *ad hoc* exercise classes, plus a bit of squash or badminton. At Prescoed, I didn't know before I got here that they had a football team. When I got here, I thought a couple of the guys were pulling my leg. Turned out, we arrived on the Friday, but Tuesday we were training on the pitch. It appeared through the woods and I thought, "Christ, it's true!" We were like kids at Christmas. We hadn't kicked a ball on grass for three years in closed conditions. All that time then there I was walking through this wonky path, through woodland. I thought it was a wind up, then you see these two pretty decent pitches. I was like, "Wow! Ok, fair enough."

I never really thought of it before, but the reason I think football works here is that you can't see the prison from the pitches, which is a really interesting point. For that ninety minutes or three hours you're down there, you're not in prison, and that's genuine. Sometimes you have to remind yourself you are in prison when it gets a bit heated on the pitch, you know, testosterone running about. But it's a small price to pay for having that ninety minutes of competitive football with your mates. I've only known guys for two or three months, but on that pitch it was true. You're there as a collective having a game of football with your mates. I get a kick out of the team dynamic, you see. All for one, one for all, sort of thing.

I've played football all my life. When I left school, [I] played at county level, played at Welsh league level, then dropped down a bit as I got older. I was centre-mid, centre-back, I'll probably be in goal by the time I'm forty! It's in the team, the dressing room mentality. It's about the banter. Saturday is brilliant, because in the morning there's banter flying around camp. I haven't had that for three or four years. It's real good. Then during the match and even after the game, up until eight or nine at night, we're still talking about missed tackles, missed opportunities. You know I said that for ninety minutes you aren't in prison? Well, even when you get back to the main camp here, the banter and discussions and missed opportunities, we have heated arguments, all in good jest, as like you would down the pub with the lads after a game on a Saturday. We chat about it all night on the wings.

I got lucky when I came here. A couple of the boys had come from C------. John and me were on the same wing there and he'd been here before; in fact, he's captain of the team now. The induction orderly grabbed us both because he knew we played and he told us about the football. The Orderly collared us and said, "Training is on Tuesday, and there's a match on Saturday, so grab some boots and pads from the training rooms and chuck 'em on!" So that was it and we got involved.

But then I didn't play right away and it's a sore point with me. It took four or five weeks, which was bloody annoying because I'm not used to being sub. It was like being twenty-one again. I'm thirty-seven and I did throw my toys out of the pram!

I didn't play at first and it was annoying. I'd train on a Tuesday and by Friday find out I'm on the bench again. At first, I thought, "Stuff this, I'm not bothering again". But when I woke up on Saturday mornings I started to regret my decision so I went back. A couple of weeks later, for whatever reason, I'm back in the team and playing every week. It was an interesting start because I got a bit annoyed. I couldn't get my head around it to start with. But then I accepted the fact that we're a football team, not a prisoner team, because we've got additional hidden responsibilities to not go in hard because that's what they'd expect a prisoner team to do, not what a football team does.

I'm centre-back now and I've been playing in that position for ten years. I'm a fair footballer, but I do like a good old-fashioned challenge. Likewise, if I get challenged, well, I'll be the first person to shake that person's hand and say fair play. But I got told to calm down a bit on the pitch. It's quite interesting, because we're a prisoner team, but we can't be going in rough. At first, I didn't think of us as a football team; I thought we were a prisoner football team. But then one of the gym officers explained things to me and put me on the bench, which I couldn't understand at first, which is why I got upset. He said, "You're too rash, so don't go in too hard, you need to stay on your feet".

At first, I didn't get it. I'm not dirty by any stretch of the imagination, but my managers before have never said go easy on another player because if I can get the ball and if I can take the player off the ball too then I'm going to try and do that. We aren't professional footballers, so if I see a ball and I can put a slide tackle in then I'm going to go for it.

I've got football boots on, it's a football pitch and we're a football team, [but] we've got a hidden responsibility as well. I imagine the opposition team are saying in their team talk to go and kick crap out of them because they can't touch you. The team knows that if we touch you they're getting this opportunity to play football removed. From our point of view, we're a team who has never said let's go and kick ten shits out of the opposition, that's never happened. I'm a centre-back doing a centre-back's job and I might go in hard. I have to reign myself in because we are a team in a prison and we don't want to give the league any reason to question our inclusion in the league. So now I absolutely understand that side; it just took a while to get used to it.

It took a while, you know. It was adapting my head to playing as a centre-back in the team, inside of the prison camp, though you feel like you're not in prison for that time. Its unspoken restrictions about what you can and cannot do. It does not exist for the opposition and it does not exist in normal football.

The boys in the football team have three sets of rulebooks to follow: football, prison and then you've got the rules that the Gym Officers tell us like staying on your feet. The trouble is they're often conflicting. You've got football rules – win that ball at any cost. Then you've got to win that ball at any cost, but not going in hard because that's breaking that rule, so it's hard. Which rule do I go for? They often overlap and contradict each other too. It's finding the balance where you can tick all three. Keep the team happy by putting the shift in, keep the staff happy and keep the prison happy too. It took me five weeks to understand that.

I've seen other players go through that too, like with John. He's played every match and he's probably the standout player in the team. He's a good footballer and he bloody knows it as well! Many a time I've had to grab him when he's gone and ignored rule book number one, the prison rules, and he's gone in too hard. He'll be effing and jeffing if the referee blows his whistle. I've had a word and said, "John, we need you on the pitch here, and by the way Mr So and So is watching so be careful." He gets immersed. Say I'm one hundred percent in; well, he's one hundred and ten percent in! Instead, I give ninety-five percent myself, so I've got five percent that is thinking about the rules because you've got to tick that box. But he's just football, football, football, which I think is brilliant, but there are two other rule books that are hovering over you. A few other boys are like that, like Paul. He's just the same because he's an ex-pro. He's probably used to the other rules from his clubs on that side of things, so it might be a bit easier for him as he's lived the game. I've just played park football. The highest I got was Welsh League, which is a good standard, but that was maybe ten years ago and there are a couple of other guys like me. Then you've got the other guys in the team who are just quiet and doing their job. It's a good, eclectic mix. I would say of the starting eleven there would be four of us that probably struggle with the other bits as well, but we deal with it in our own way.

Always reflect after the game on what could I have done differently. That's just my own sporting head. I missed that tackle, I could have stood him up there, you know. Before the match I tell myself to stay on my feet. When I first had the disagreement about what you can and cannot do, in the end I thought, well, I want to play, so I'll just go with it. Spent the first couple of games on my feet, didn't have a good game, so I got brought off. I'm used to my manager saying, "When that number ten gets past you, I want you to absolutely clatter him, go through him". That's what I'm used to being told; now it's "Stand him up, try and drag him out of position". Changing the game that way.

The lads playing football here are dispersed all across camp so there's no sort of collective football unit. Within two weeks I made some good mates, a few acquaintances and then you get to know them, nods across camp. Now it doesn't feel like prison at all. It helped me get into the team; Tuesday training, there's a buzz around camp. You see lads gearing themselves up for it.

The first couple of nights here, I played pool with a couple of lads and got to know two or three faces. In a football training session you might get ten, fifteen, twenty people that you are playing with. There are handshakes afterwards, so that's the initial contact made. Then on camp you see them and nod your head. Next week they are asking if you are going to training and within a couple of weeks you've built that relationship up. That's why it was important to me, when I found out that it wasn't just a myth, the football pitch thing. When I got here, I knew quite a few faces, from C------, so I knew quite a few boys here. This is my first and last time in prison, so it's not as if I'd been here before. What do I do best is I socialise, to go and have a kick about to meet new people. So the football was really good for me coming in like that.

It's like when I was younger. The twenty-four-year-old me moved in with my then girlfriend, to an area near her hometown. There was football pitch behind the house and I found out who played there. So, walking the dog, I watched a few games but didn't speak to anybody. I thought it was a bloody good standard and they were all my age as well. After a while I approached the manager and we got chatting. I found out when they trained and he asked me if I played a bit and who for. He knew a few managers who knew me, so he phoned them and they said I was a tidy centre-back. So I started training with them, then started going drinking and socialising with them because everybody knows everybody's business there. When you're in that mix and not knowing everybody's business, you stick out like a sore thumb. So, I made it my business to get involved in the mix and by playing football it worked perfectly. Within a month I went to a couple of training sessions and had a couple of minutes on the pitch. I was an outsider coming in, so I had to ease my way in, but before long I was starting every game. That helped me integrate into that little community, and the parallels here with the community at Prescoed, it's exactly the same. Moved here, started training. It's almost an acceptance to a close-knit community, it's almost like a central focus point. Up the valleys, it'd be rugby, but around here football is the one that does it.

I'm not a Gym Orderly because I don't want to go round cleaning up after people. I've got a couple of training partners but my thing though is diet and healthy eating, alongside the gym. That's been my mainstay for the last fifteen years. Went off the rails a bit the last three years before I come here with the drink and a little bit of cocaine. Booze took over my life for five years to the point where, if this hadn't happened to me, going to prison, I wouldn't have seen forty. So now I've got my gym back, my healthy eating, I'm watching my protein and my carbs. A bit of OCD about it, but I've hit my calorie target and my gains, but that's my thing. So, gym, education and football for me. Like one of the lads said, it's like Butlins but without the booze! It is what you make of it in here. I'm re-educating myself, I'm hitting the gym hard and I'm clean eating. People moan about the food here, but you can supplement you're diet very easy if you know what you're doing.

Football plays a big part in how I set out my week. Saturday, it's a whole session pretty much from the morning banter until nine or ten o'clock when the banter finishes. Saturday is football day like it was on the out. There's a massive parallel between football outside and in here, except we're not pissed at the end of the day! And on that note, because we don't drink here, we're probably one of the fittest teams in the league, you see the other teams gassing out and you think five or six years ago that was probably us, but the dedication and the fitness is another key thing for us. When we finish some of the boys will run laps of the camp and some go and work out. I can't see any Saturday teams on the outside going back in the gym!
Sport In prison for me comes down to the fitness aspect. When I see the other team gassing after the first half (and you should see the shape and size of half of them, no disrespect, because I've been there) you should see our team coming through, not just myself, but our collective team powering through. It's not just to the last minute either because we have some left in the tank.

On Sunday morning I'll be up doing ten laps which is roughly five k at a walk, maybe go to gym Sunday afternoon with a couple of the boys. On Tuesdays we train for a couple of hours then hit the gym doing a leg day or a chest day. On the out, I didn't finish training and go to the gym. I finished training and then went and had a couple of beers or got a Chinese in. It's almost like a professional mentality, we're keeping ourselves fit.

It all part and parcel of my life now. I've still got ten months left and [the] gym is back in my life. To be fair, I thought because I hadn't played football properly for two or three years I thought I might be too old to play. But, actually, I've got a couple of years left in me, and I've still got a few tricks up my sleeve. When I get out in October I'll be looking to carry on playing and making a few calls to old contacts, saying I've got a couple of seasons left in me, so how about giving me a shot? Had I not come in here I probably wouldn't have bothered playing football again. My first couple of games I was blowing out of both ends thinking this is hard work, but now the fitness is coming on, diet is bang on, and by the end I'm hardly breaking a sweat.

If I hadn't come inside I wouldn't have seen forty. At my trial, my GP said that and the psychiatrist said that. When I came in I thought I was in good shape. I was sixteen and a half stone. I'm now fourteen stone two; in the space of a year I've healthily dropped two stone. Not crash dieting, just working hard and gradually cutting all the crap out. It works both ways. You can do sitting around playing computer games and eat shit. That's there for you inside. Or you can engage in sport, re-educate yourself, keep your head ticking over, engage in football, eat healthy and go the other way. There's nobody forcing you which way to go, it's up to you. Do you just become a sloth, or do I start putting things in place for when you get out. Yeah, I wouldn't have seen forty, without a shadow of a doubt. The amount I was drinking, the amount I was stressing, the amount I ate, and that's all gone now. I never say never, but I don't want to feel the need to touch a drop of alcohol ever again. I've seen the benefits. I like the sober me. It was a while since I saw that guy, but I like it.

I can tell you my fat content, my water content, because I measure it all, that's my drive. That's not something I've suddenly acquired, that's something I used to do years and years ago. I've got my mojo back. I couldn't put it better than that. I can tell you how many grams of protein I put in my body yesterday for goodness sake! One hundred and eighty-four grams. I usually put two hundred in, but I just couldn't face any more tuna!

The education and the gym was all that was happening when I was in HMP C------. Football still happened, but five-a-side on the Astroturf is alright for a kick about but it's not football. You can't put your sliding tackles in so it's not the same. You make your own choices when you come in, especially in D Cat, because you're expected to survive, as it's the next step before you get out. In closed, you are told what to do. That was difficult, but some people need that. When you get to D Cat, if you want a doctor's appointment, you go and make a doctor's appointment. You go and find your own way. There's a couple of guys like me when they come in; they'll help you out. I would have still done the education because my CV is a bit knackered at the minute, so I need to look at different avenues to support me for the next twenty years of my working life. The gym definitely would have happened, it's not cardiovascular, but it's not a good adrenaline rush. You see your gains, but it's a separate part of your mind. I love the football; you don't get the banter in the gym. You don't get the team aspect. In the gym, you do your own thing, you have a training buddy, but you are there for your own gain.

Education keeps me engaged upstairs. The big thing for me at the minute, from an educational perspective, is the CHASE Programme, and I'm doing Advice and Guidance Level 3 with St Giles Trust, Understanding Mental Health Level 3 with Prisoners Education Trust, plus I'm doing a bit of psychology work and I go gym every day.

I think for me personally, when you've got the education, when you've got the gym, when you've got the football, every box is being ticked. When I start getting my ROTLs and I get to see my family then it's done. It's just a case of seeing the next ten months out now. I don't mean just existing; I mean positively seeing the next ten months out. I'm playing football on weekends and training once a week like I used to. I'm going to the gym every other day like I used to. I'm retraining my mind like I used to. I'm not drinking but I used to. It's all the good stuff, minus the crap.

I won't touch drink. I will try not to touch drink again in my life because it's not good for me. From a physical aspect and a mental rehabilitation aspect, I know it. I'll play ninety minutes and I do not gas out. Then I go to the gym and train for an hour, do ten laps and be fine. I like that I have that longevity in me that I can go and do stuff, not get hammered by having three or four pints, sit down, TV on, etc. It's given me that health awareness as well. As far as rehabilitation goes, football, gym, and education are all of equal importance to me for different reasons.

Paul

That's what got me through prison, just playing football every day.

Defence
Kitchen Orderly

I'm Paul, thirty-six, I'm in prison for selling drugs. I left professional football in 2001. I didn't have any solid qualifications, so I just did jobs that I knew how to do. I had my own business buying and selling houses, but I lost a lot of it at the start of 2009 when my wife had cancer and we lost a lot of money and houses whilst she was ill. So I decided to go back to college about four or five years ago and get my bricklaying qualifications. In doing so I was only on a hundred and fifty pound[s] a week. I went to find an easy way of making extra money for the family. Due to that, selling drugs, I got caught [and] I ended up back in prison.

Some people go and do it and I had my own reason. People can judge. I knew I was breaking the law. I made that decision. I felt for me it was the right reason at the time, and obviously I'm being punished, and my family are being punished as well. It's a double-edged sword really.

I was in HMP S------ before here for six and a half months. I've been inside before. I was in for violence back in 2003. I stayed clear of all that since then. I learnt my lesson. Just a bit young and when I finished football my head was all over the shop. I went back there this time and boxed clever for a while.

I was playing for the youth for my local professional club at about eleven or twelve years old. I played in a friendly against a club in London when I was fourteen and they signed me. Done my youth teams at ages fourteen, fifteen and sixteen with them. That meant every weekend and holiday I was in London, which is quite tough as a teenager, living with strange people and that. Then I had an opportunity because they let me go and I could sign for a couple of northern clubs or my local professional club. I had to play a trial game for each of them, but after the game for the local professional club, myself and my friends were offered a contract. The club said we had to sign for them and they didn't want us to play anywhere else. If I had gone and played in another trial game that weekend and they had heard about it then they would have taken the contract offer away. They said it's sign now or you don't sign. Being away from my family for two years at that given moment I decided to stay at home and sign.

Did my apprenticeship with them then scholarships, international scholarships, caps at fourteen, sixteen and eighteen. Just before I finished my apprenticeship, I managed to make two appearances for the first team, so that sealed my professional contract. But there were still coaches that didn't want me to be there, against the manager and his assistants, who were ex-professional, [with] a bit more knowledge, [and] they wanted me to sign. So they said we'll give you a six-month contract to see how you go.

But in that six months my mates got involved in a fight. I was there, got into trouble and got brought into it. It was all over the papers: "Football Star in Vicious Assault", and that was it: they terminated my contract after two months.

After that I got signed by a club in Northamptonshire and I went straight up there because my cousin was playing for them. I got a flat, my wife was just pregnant with my first child, and we were going to make a home up there. When I came home one weekend and got into a fight I contracted septicaemia in my hand because I bust my knuckles up. So I was out for six, seven months and was then let go by the club. I came up to the Welsh league, played for everyone in the premier in the South Wales region, Division one, Division two, and just local league football to get a bit of love back in the sport.

I'm one of the few ones here for whom football was their job, and that's not the case for many people. But if anyone's got an interest or a passion for football like myself and they turn up to training, it's still for them. Being able to put boots on, go on a grass pitch and have a run round on a Tuesday, it still makes them feel like it's detached from the prison. It's not like you're looking back at the prison. You're just in a park and I feel that physically. Walking away from here and being alone on that pitch, you could be anywhere really; in your local park or anywhere. They didn't plan it like that, but that's where the pitches are and that's what it feels like. It's a good thing. And the pitch, at the start of the season, is unbelievable, and it's almost like a cup final pitch! It's a treat to play on a pitch that flat and surrounded by such scenery.

I love football. That's what got me through prison, just playing football every day. I'd heard about the team here and I was really excited to try and find out what the level was like. I'd heard that a lot of ex-pros had come through the system and had played for them. They played a really good standard, so although I was really excited to come up, I was nervous too, to be honest. If I needed to, I knew I could play in goals. My level, my standard, would be better than what keepers they would have. I was hoping that wouldn't happen and I could play out. As I'm getting older, I enjoy running about and doing a bit more exercise. I'd prefer to be in the thick of the action.

I landed here on a Wednesday, so the boys I knew said we've got to get you in the team. The first game was on the Saturday, so I managed to get in as a ball boy, to see the standard and what the boys were like. There were some good players and there still is, but the standard they played against was a little bit less. The score was 19-1 so it made it look a bit easy. I saw the keeper, and I could play in goal, but I set my sights on playing out. Next week was training on Tuesday and the game after that I was sub.

The weekends are the hardest time in prison. A weekend banged up is horrendous. As a Gym Orderly I managed to get out a bit, but it's a strict regime on the weekend, banged up from half-past four, an hour out, no work or nothing. You're in your cell all day and then you're in from four-thirty until the morning. You can't speak to your family after four-thirty, so it's hard. You only got a visit in S------ if we were lucky. But here we get visits, so I try and plan them on a Sunday. Football on a Saturday fills your weekend up and for two hours you're not a prisoner, you're free from everything. That's the way I've always looked at football. If I've been really upset, I'm still getting out of prison for that hour and a half to switch off, no worries in the world. I'm on the pitch and it's the end of it.

There's a lot of similarities to my time playing for the club in London when I played professionally. Spending time away at weekends and holidays. That's the reason why I took to prison quite comfortably; [it] is because I had to go away, spend a lot of time away from home and family when I was younger. It does hurt me a bit to think back. It's hard work to go and play football, people don't realise. Then when you're just let go by the club, people don't realise the hard work you put in; it just gets taken away from you. It's mad.

In Prescoed, I'm in the kitchens. I have a love for food. It's another little passion of mine and it's another thing that passes time. I work hard, spend as much time as I can there. The only time I like to leave is to go to the gym or football. I like to work into the night, go to badminton, then go to sleep. So, it's just work, sport, sleep, work, sport, sleep. That's the best way to fill my time. It's all I do is to try and fill it with either work or sport. I play table tennis as well, anything sports related. Football is the main one, but on record I'm the best in the prison at badminton and table tennis! I am competitive in whatever I do. It's good to be competitive. I never started off the best at any of them, but I've worked hard just to make myself better.

For me, if there were five days of football, I would play five days of football. I only go to the gym to train because you can't do the football every day here. It would have been different if there was no team here; you would have had to get on with it, but the weekend would be drawn out. You haven't got work and you've got to find something to do. It helps the boys with problems with drugs or getting up to no good. Not only do you get punished here, if you get caught doing something bad then you get kicked out. But because they've got football they're not bored. For me, personally, I feel that it is just living for the weekends. I look forward to them so much now. I never looked forward to the weekends at S------.

On the out as well, when I play in my team, I'm a senior figure. I'm thirty-six, not many are still playing then, but I'm club captain and still seen as a role model, and when it comes to things, I will automatically take things on and have a chat. Like with one of the new boys the other day after his first game with us. He's just come in and I said to keep coming to training, he'd done well, and that he'll get in the team. He was sub in the first game and training on the Tuesday. We need him really.

Football's helped me with a lot of self-control. I have got a lot of passion and I do get carried away sometimes. It's not just out there on the pitch where we can get in trouble. It continues when you go back into the prison. So, self-control, things like encouraging people, seeing people around and trying to be a bit more helpful.

All I want to do, when I'm in here, I'm trying to get help with work back as a bricklayer on the out. Just got qualified a year before I come into prison. The plan I had before coming in here got ripped up and thrown in my face pretty much. It was a bit of a panic at first, "What am I going to do?" I decided to relax and leave it be, take care of each day as it comes and eventually I will end up going home. If I stay in work, the good side to that is that I get to train every day. There's positives and negatives in everything but I keep trying to look at the positives and going home soon will fill me with so much happiness, so I think when I come back it will give me a little boost then. Football games will kick off again; we've not had a game for a while and it feels like I'm missing out.

My wife doesn't look forward to me playing. She says I've been with her for twenty-three years, since we've been thirteen, and every Saturday has always been about football. She's asked if maybe she could have some Saturdays when I come out. I did point out though that I'm home four months of the year in the summer, when I don't have football, but they forget about that part! I did say that I'll take my little one over for her; he's football crazy. Take him along with me then and give her a bit of a break.

I'm passionate for teaching kids to play football. I had my coaching badge for years. My wife nagged me to do some toddler football groups and I should have listened to her. I couldn't commit to it, and with some of the charges I've had, I've been negative about it, that they wouldn't want me. But even with all this negativity, she always pushed me to do it. Maybe even if it's just starting a football team up for my son and do the coaching. I'd need my sports leaders and my coaching badges and I may be able to get some help with it when I get out. That to me would mean everything.

With regards to bricklaying and all that, I've got my qualifications. But if it's something to do with the football coaching and that, I would be more happy with that rather than my first A-Level or manual handling. I would prefer that. It would give me that little kick-start to go, "Right. Okay. I can go get my next badge." I can get funding from the PFA because I played, but it's like getting yourself to go round and do everything. It might be an option when I come out. I've got my tag at the end of March, so only three and a half months left. My first home leave is soon so I can go home and spend the weekend with my family before Christmas.

Calum

In here you try and keep it in, you learn not to just fly off the rails.

Defender

So, I've been in prison now for four years and I've got sixteen months left. Date's etched in my brain. I can't wait for that date. I'm in for drugs. First and only time I've been in prison. Got a couple of kids. That's it really.

Been playing for the football team six months now, since I come up here. Before that, I used to play at HMP P--- as well. There it was gym every morning, seven until eight. Plus, I'd do circuits, football and played badminton. Just keeping busy, right.

When I first went in, it was to HMP C------ for fourteen or fifteen months. I was on remand for eleven months, got sentenced. Then I was on hold then because I was a listener. When the six months was up, I got sent to P---. I don't know, I'd never been anywhere else, so I thought it was just prison. I was gutted to go to be honest, but after a couple of weeks, I loved it there. As far as prison goes, it's the best you're going to get. Some places are dirty and you're banged up all the time. The gym isn't very good and football is only twice a week. There you get gym every day, plus circuits, so really you can get to the gym twice a day, football three or four times a week and football competitions all the time, so it was good.

In jail, I've worked as a cleaner, servery and as a listener. I enjoyed it. I think it's about two and a half years I've done it for – being a listener. I didn't mind doing it – sometimes you get woken up early, but I didn't mind. I'm one of the quieter guys here, but I always take everything in. In a funny way, I've always been a listener like that. I get to hear everything that's going on.

Before I came to Prescoed I knew a little about the football here, but only from people who have got sent back from here. They would say you can play football, not much more really. I didn't know it was a league just that teams come in from outside, really. But they told me it was a grass pitch, eleven a side. And you get some good players up here, people who have played pro and different things. They keep winning and they never lose! That was it.

I haven't played football since I was at school and I'm in my thirties now. I like to keep myself fit. I've always been into gym, but football? I just didn't have time before. I have kids, I was busy working, I was self-employed, and so you can't play on a weekend.

So when I came here, I got involved straight away. To me it was just about keeping busy. Especially when you're stuck on camp it makes the time go quicker. Stops you thinking about the outside; you forget about it for an hour or two. So the first chance I had, I borrowed some boots. They weren't the best, but it was my first session, so I didn't mind.

It was alright back in the summer playing. Couple of times we had fourteen or fifteen a side back in the summer. All the fair-weather footballers come out, whereas in the winter you're lucky to get ten! So because I'd been training over the summer, they picked me for the first game of the season this September.

One of the other things, one of the positives of coming here [is] that I'm closer to family, town visits and working out. Although I don't like it, because it's boring, it is work. I'm getting back to normal. Then in six months I'll get my home leaves as well.
They had a family day here the other week. Some of the men brought their families up to watch them play. But when I first heard about it, I thought they were messing around, someone taking the piss! I'd like to get that chance though, just for my kids really. My boy played football, but since I've been in, he's stopped going now. My partner is working all the time, so it's hard work.

When football comes round, I can't wait until a Saturday. You go and have a little bit of fun. Now I play football on a Saturday and have a town visit on a Sunday, so the weekend just goes. Time does go quick like that. The football helps with the weeks, it really does. When there's not a game you're gutted because you're sat on your bed. When there's a game the afternoon goes quick.

It's interesting too where the football pitches are located. It's away from the camp, so that you can't see the prison when you are there. You forget where you are. I suppose you forget you're in prison. Football's like that. Even when I was playing in the other prison, you are inside the walls but you just forget where you are. Takes me back to when I was playing football as a kid on the Astroturf. It's the only thing that helps time to go quicker in here.

Helps you get to know people too. You get talking to people, meet people when you're on the same team as them. You're not going to say, "What's your name?", but when you're playing you're talking to each other all the time. When I came up here, I knew quite a few of the boys because I've been in for so long. A lot of people come here from P---, so you know a good few boys. That helps with the settling in. You can ask people, "How do I do this, how do I do that?"

Playing in the team here, you've got to do things for others if you want the team to succeed. It's hard work sometimes, especially if you've got someone who only plays [with] their friends. You've got to put up with it and even with the coaches, whoever it is, you've got to put up with that. Doesn't matter if it's Prescoed or somewhere else. But you'll always find that, even when you're out, I suppose. There'll always be favourites. You'll always get it.

In the beginning I hadn't played since school, so I had to get back into it, and it was hard work sometimes because you've got a referee and different things to think about. I'm more chilled out now. Football in prison can help in a couple of ways, especially for when people get out. Some of the guys have talked about how football in prison can help them. It probably helps their discipline. If you're playing football on the out and it's a bad tackle, you'd probably start fighting. In here you try and keep it in, you learn not to just fly off the rails. Out there is a different story. People are learning that it's not all about fighting, you just get on with it.

I've waited to come up here since the day I came in. I suppose you've got to try and do things for yourself here, whereas when you're in closed, you've got to get up when they tell you to. They tell you to go to work, and if you haven't gone, they ask you why. They're mothering you. Here, if you've got to go to healthcare, then you've got to go to healthcare. You've got to do things for yourself.

Some of the staff here with the football, they help give some of the young boys who need it a little push. It's helped a few, made them a bit more confident, maybe. It's helped them get to meet people like myself. Helped them get to know people's names.

When I got to Prescoed I wanted to learn a trade for when I get out. First place I went to, it didn't work out. That's why I left. I need to do something and I want to learn. Now I'm working but just labouring and it's boring. It's wasted time, even though you you're earning money. I'm going to look for something else. I want to be out of camp working, but I want to get something out of it, where I'm going to learn. That's why I did carpentry when I was in P---. So, when I come up here, I wanted to carry it on to get a little bit of experience. That's why I want to get something new. Like a lot of the boys here, employment is your main focus because you're making money. I've got kids and I've been away four years.

I doubt I'll keep playing when I'm out because I'll be working hard, though I would like to. If it's a Saturday or Sunday and training through the week, plus working every day with a couple of kids. It'll be five and half years I'll have been away for in total, to make up for. So it'll be nice to take my lad down the park and watch football, even go and watch him play. For me, there'll not be enough hours in the day for that.

If there hadn't been any football here, it probably would have been a bit boring. Especially if you aren't into the gym, there's nothing you can do up here. The education side of things is not for a lot of boys. It would have made my time go slower. But now if it's a Wednesday you're just waiting for Saturday, for the game. Just looking forward to something all the time. It gives you some optimism. I want to pass that on to my kids to just get on with it, to get back up, go out and enjoy it. It is good even though I haven't done if for so long.

In school I played all the way through but I didn't play for any team when I came out. I was a county-level swimmer and when I was in school, I didn't play for a team because

I was swimming six times a week with competitions on the weekend. I was training first thing before school, probably six o'clock till eight-thirty, three times a week, and in the evenings then probably about six-thirty till nine. I didn't have time for football. I enjoyed it in the beginning, but towards the end I got fed up of it, and when I was about sixteen or seventeen I'd had enough. I'd got a girlfriend by then and I didn't want to swim any more.

That experience taught me a lot. When I was swimming, I was made to go by my dad who was pushing me and pushing me. I didn't enjoy it. So if my boy wanted to get into a sport and then if he wanted to quit, I would let him, otherwise he's not going to enjoy it, when he's being made to do it. You've got to allow him to make his own mind up.

One of the things football gives you here is that it gives you enjoyment. I think that if you're pushed, you're not going to give it your best. That's one of the successes of the team here; they all enjoy it. You may get some of them arguing after the first five minutes and you just think come on boys, just enjoy it, it's not the premier league. Just enjoy it.

Neil

You use your team like a family. You know they're going to be there for you.

Midfield

I'm a Valleys boy, doing a nine-year sentence for class A drugs and a firearm. I'm coming to the end of it; I've got about ten weeks left. So, happy days, I can't wait. This is my third time in prison, but my second time for drugs. First time was back when I was fifteen; that was a violence charge. It was a while ago.

I'm coming to the end of my time here now. Obviously, when you start, you think it's never going to get here, but it's come round and it feels that it's gone quick. It probably doesn't sound like it to someone on the outside. Four and a half years to someone out there is a good while, but when you're in here you've got your routines to stick to, so that when you look back you realise that's helped time to go quick.

I spent time C------, P--- and P-------, for three and a half years. That was back when jail was jail. You didn't have televisions. All you had to do was reading and that's where I learnt to write tidy. I just picked it up from different things around me. I've got very neat handwriting because I used to see people with different writing, and some writing looks nice. So I copied it from their style and that's just the way I've ended up writing now.

I've got a couple of GCSEs but nothing special. I'll never know what I had because in the gap between finishing my GCSEs and leaving school there's two or three weeks where I ended up doing what I did. So I never knew how I'd done because by then I was in jail.

I played a bit of sport in prison. At C------ you get to have a little game of football once or twice a week. You get to use the gym, get back a bit of fitness. Back in P-------, because it was all youngsters, you've got to keep them more productive. They are YOs and we'd have little five–a-side competitions. When I first went to P---, their pitch was a concrete one, so I used to go through a pair of trainers so quickly. You don't want to come down on that hard surface! We'd do a lot of circuits. If you want to get fit in jail the opportunity is there. But in C------ now you're lucky to get in the gym three times a week. At P--- and in here you can pretty much do it every day. There I was a Gym Orderly, so I was working in the gym too. You'd do touch rugby, circuits, badminton, wall climbing, weights, football, you can do a good few things there. Up here, you're only allowed one weight session a day, but you can do a CV [cardio-vascular] routine if you got one. We're lucky as well, we've got football. But a little bit of touch rugby would be alright up here as well.

I knew about the football team before I came here from some of the boys in the other prisons who'd been there that I knew. So it was always something I was going to go for. Also, I knew they had a pretty good record. There's always been decent players up here and even though the boys are in jail, most of us have done sports before we went inside when we were younger.

Some boys who have been on heroin, some of the boys, they don't look too clever, but stick them on the football field and they're a different person. It's just like you never forget how to ride a bike; that stuff stays with you. All of us probably went through school and we've all done sports, so it's stuck with us, and even though we turned to crime, we've still got that sporting background behind us. Most jails do football, but it's usually just a five-a-side pitch, or you're playing against each other. Up here you've got the opportunity where you are in the league, so that's something different. Something not many jails offer.

I wanted to come here because it was an open prison. I've always liked football and it can help because if I want to get out and play again, you've got a head start. You're match fit, you can go out and get straight into it. Not every jail does that. If you're playing on Astroturf or concrete and then when you run around on grass for an hour and a half it's totally different, especially on a soggy day. It's a different fitness, a different game.

I'll be working when I get out. I'll try and find time to play for someone, but I'm not sure who yet. So we'll see where it is and it will depend what hours I work, see what happens. I don't want to chuck it in before I get too old. I'm thirty-eight this year.

I played one or two games at the end of last season when I first came to Prescoed, then all of this season apart from times I've had home leaves. Pretty much since I got here in the April. We're a good bunch of boys. Obviously, you've got that team building thing going, so you're not thinking about yourself and you're not working one day a week. You might be on camp, but you're training Tuesdays. You're not just thinking about yourself at that point because it's a team game. In the past, out of the team, they've had five or six superstars; this season we're more of a team. No one stands out like they have in the past. So, as a new team, we probably play a bit better football. We click, we actually use all our players.

Trouble is we can't go up or down, which is a shame, because obviously, some of the games we have, the teams aren't pushing us at all. You've got to plod along with them and some of the teams drag us down. It happened once this season. We weren't playing the best of teams, but they just got in our heads and we ended up losing. It was the first loss in three seasons.

In fact, losing that one game made us better, even though that hurt us. Being the team that lost once in so many seasons, we don't want that to happen again, and we can't wait to have them again next month. We've got to go out and prove a point now, which we have done the games after, where we played back-to-basics football. For some teams, their supporters can help them, but we don't have that. In the jail, you've got the ref, and the opposition have got all their people on the side-line, calling out, and helping a decision go their way. We haven't got that, so nine times out of ten decisions go against us. They know we've beaten them by this score or that score, so we tend to give them the benefit of the doubt anyway.

Half the time, our gym officers are refereeing the game and they've got to make it as fair as they can. If he's at one end of the pitch he can't really be calling the offside rule. You're at the other end of the field with the ball and because they have all those people on their side, and they're all shouting for it, he's going to give it to them anyway.

From last season I think there's only me and Jermaine left. Last season you had certain players who were part of a clique always passing to each other. It wasn't so much of a team game. They wanted the ball passed straight to them and they tried to win games on their own, and it worked for them. But this season has been much better. A lot more boys have come in, and although we haven't had as much training because of the weather, not many people know who our big players are. We've got a settled team pretty much, but anyone who wants to turn up, they'll still put them on the bench. It's pretty much a brand-new team.

It's surprising at training, because of the numbers of the people working out off camp, we don't actually do proper training, which I think is what we should be doing. We'll just go over with twelve to fourteen people, pick two teams and have a game of football. There's not much training going on. So our first game as a team, when went out there and being a brand-new team, we didn't' know how it was going to go. The first ten to fifteen minutes we were finding our feet and then we ended up winning twelve one!

That side is still the same now. Whoever was there at the start of the season, you've got the odd one or two who will be out working. There are still new boys coming in, plus a couple of injuries, home visits and working, but there's always potential for people to turn up and have a game.

Last game, a couple of the families come in on a visit to watch us play. Perhaps that might help a bit because the boys want to perform a bit better in front of their families. It was a really good thing, but the only way you're going to find out is by keeping doing it. It's an open jail. Some spend five days home with their family anyway. It shouldn't do no harm once every few games; they do family days anyway. It shouldn't be an issue. It will be nice for the boys with kids for their kids to come in and see their dads play.

Prisons can be selfish places, especially if you are in closed conditions. You've got to look after yourself and then you come to an open prison where you've got to think about things a little differently. You're responsible for making those decisions, whereas before someone made them for you. It's like with the family day. I'd rather the boys who have got kids, to let them have it, there's no point in a mate or a cousin of mine coming up.

Let the boys who actually need it use it. I think about myself all week, so an hour and a half won't hurt, will it?

No one wants to get sent back to a closed prison and there's a lot you've got to think about. That's the thing here, some of the teams when they come up to play us, they're a bit wary at first because they don't know what we're in for. But they can get away with a lot of stuff with us that we can't. If we get into an argument then anything could happen, because we're losing a lot more than just a red card. They don't pay a fine, the club pays the fine. But we've got to pay the fine ourselves, or could get kicked out of the jail, or they don't see their family over a little argument. They can be a little bit dirty with us, the other teams; you've just got to bite your tongue and get on with it. We do get dragged down a level sometimes, but the best way we can beat them is just playing football and doing like we've been doing, scoring these fifteen nil or nineteen one scores we've been getting. That sends out more of a message really than giving someone a clip.

I'm a pretty calm guy. When I want something, I know I can go and do it, I can go and get it, like the job I've got for when I'm released. I'm all ready to go down there. Hopefully, that's the one that's going to keep me out of trouble. I'm not a prolific offender I've only done what I had to do, basically to survive. I didn't want to do it. I've always worked. It's when I haven't been working, I have ended up selling drugs. But last time I had an accident. I had to have an operation and because I was self-employed I wasn't entitled to anything. So when I got out of hospital, everything I'd worked hard for to get, like my own place and all that, it was in my head that I couldn't afford to keep it. So I went back to what I knew, and that was something I shouldn't have done. But I thought at the time that I had to do it.

I could always go back to my old line of work [construction], but I've done a couple of qualifications now, so I don't want to be outside on a building site in all weathers. I'd rather be working and be doing something different. I've got a couple of personal training qualifications, I've got a job in a gym waiting for me when I get out, nice big gym, so the world is my oyster again.

Playing against the opposition, against outside teams, it can bring problems. I've lost my head in games out there, but you've got to learn to be calm about it. The best way to get them back is to just beat them on the pitch. Go back to basics. Do what we do. That's more in their face than shouting at them. You can use that in everyday life, can't you?

The gym is my main thing in here. I love football anyway because of the fitness thing, I'm one of the oldest out there, but I'm probably one of the fittest too. That's part of my cardio sessions. The gym, I'm into CrossFit too, a real all-rounder. Everyone wants to be the best at what they do. I'm still competitive, so it's not a bad thing knowing you're the fittest guy out there. I see sport as another fitness session for me.

Sport teaches you things. You're not thinking about yourself, you've got to think of the bigger picture, and especially when you are out there, the world doesn't revolve around you. You can try and make it do that, but obviously it's not going to. The more people around you, the better things are for you. A problem shared is a problem halved. Knowing you have people around you can rely on. People out there have got their family, they might not talk to them as much, but you can still use them the same. You use your team like a family. You know they're going to be there for you.

Don't get me wrong, we all like to have a laugh as soon as we're in the changing room, getting ready for a game or whatever. We still have banter, but we know we have to go out and do what we have to do. So there's nothing wrong with giving someone a bit of constructive criticism, you're only helping them out at the end of the day. People don't take it too serious when you give them a bit of guidance. It seems to work for us.

It goes back to the personal fitness training I've done. If someone comes up to me and says they need to be able to do this in a certain amount of time, they've got to be willing to put the hours in and listen to what I say, otherwise they're not going to reach their goal. I know what people need to do to get to where they want to be. If people don't want to listen, I can't make them listen. If you give them constructive criticism and they don't take it, well, that's their choice. If people don't want to change, they aren't going to, you've got to want to do it for yourself. You need to take things on board. The boys are saying it because they know that it's right. They're not going to say it if it's wrong.

For me, I wouldn't say it would make that much of a difference if the football wasn't here, it just gives you something to look forward to. Some boys, they do love their football through and through. That might be the only reason they keep their head down in closed conditions to come up here. For me, it's the gym side of it. I want to be out and working; my job is going to come before anything else. I would have loved to be a professional footballer but that's not how it worked out.

When we play, it's like you're not in jail again. Back out, playing football, you're out of the way. It's a pitch in the middle of the woods, so you don't feel like you're in jail. Even just walking on the camp you don't feel like you're in jail because for most of us, a lot of us, we served time in closed conditions. We're used to being on the wings, seeing the walls around you, barbed wire. Up here, all that's gone straight away. There's hardly anything holding you back. You can just be you. That's what sets you back up for release.

When you first get up here it is a bit weird, still walking round the path at night. You're not back on the wing like someone who has done nine years. You think to yourself, what the fuck's going on here? Reminded me of my first sentence. I'd been in three and a half years and I was only young. It was a bit of a shock. I wasn't used to certain things like going in a shop and ordering food, handing money over. None of that happens in jail. It's all done for you. Fill in a piece of paper and it comes to you. Here, you end up working off camp and it helps you out. Eases you back into being outside.

Does football help? I don't know. I don't see how it would help with not reoffending. If someone has a game of football, it's up to them at the end of the day if they commit a crime or not. I can't speak for other people. I don't want to be in jail, I don't want to come back. Some people just flow through their sentence and they don't care. I've done the qualifications whenever I've been in jail, so I've always done something to help me when I get out. A lot of people don't bother doing that.

You can't even say jail will stop me reoffending because you don't know what's around the corner. Anything could happen. You could be driving a car, you crash, someone dies and you get done for that. Only you can stop yourself reoffending. If you're out now and you do play football, it's only keeping you busy for a few hours a week. What they are doing the rest of the time with their week, they need to be doing productive things: working, doing this, doing that. A job where they're earning money, so they aren't committing crime to earn money. It's up to the individual person. You can only change if you want to change.

John

When I'm on the pitch, I'm not in prison. I'm at home.

Captain
Midfielder
Education Orderly

I grew up on a big housing estate. Went to a brand new primary school as a kid. Was always playing football even then. If I didn't have a ball, I'd be kicking bottle lids and stuff. I grew up in care. I've got 3 other brothers and 2 sisters. One sister lives in London; she went to uni and never came back. My other sister has got mental health problems; she lives with my mother. One brother is a doorman, the other is unemployed. Myself though, I'm the youngest and the wisest.

Been in Prescoed four months nearly, but before this I was in HMP C------. Not my first time in prison. It's my third, but my second adult offence. I've been in Prescoed before on my second sentence. I went in jail as a kid, I was out for a bit then, and I've got two drug offences which are my adult offences.

Went into care when I was three and I was adopted with my brother at the age of fifteen, who I was with at the time. I had to change my last name. My brother was a good football player and I went to his matches; he was amazing. He used to play with some players who made it professional. Remember reading a football book in prison, a player's autobiography, and there was a picture of him in it! I wasn't aware of that until I was reading it and I told everyone, "That's my brother!"

I knew he was a good player. He was in the regionals team, schools, but he never played centre of excellence, though he was always with the best players. He was my initial inspiration as a child growing up. I'll always pay homage to that. I still speak to him and we're still close.

Playing for the school team, I was good. Not to boast, but I was good. In fact, I played two years above my age group with my brother and I used to score the goals in that team. I also used to play my own age group and one year above, so I was playing three age groups in total! My headmaster coached part-time for the centre of excellence and he put three of us into it when I was eleven. I was there for a season but didn't play many games and I found it hard travelling. Back then my stepmother didn't drive, so it was hard to get where I needed to go, whether it was Sheffield or West Brom, and there was no transport with the team. I didn't know many of the players and a lot of the players came from good backgrounds, so I didn't really mix in well. Found it hard to integrate. I remember going to my first training session and I didn't have the correct shoes, and they said normally they wouldn't let me play with them, but they gave me a chance anyway.

I don't know if it was my background or my ethnicity? Maybe because I couldn't get to the games so they weren't fussed on me, or maybe it was because I wasn't as good as the other players? It could have been a number of things, but they told me I was inconsistent. I had a letter saying we believe John is a really good player, he shines on occasions and then goes missing on others. I was a child. I was eleven at the time. That was the highest level I would have played. It stays with you that kind of thing. I remember training with the size two balls, I remember it all.

Carried on playing locally at under twelves and under fourteens, but I stopped playing when I was fifteen. I left care then due to a disagreement and I went to live with my brother. We had a flat together, but really, my life started to spiral from there. No structure, no father, no mother, whatever I saw my brother do, I wanted to do it too. I stopped going to school then even though it was a good school. Didn't do my GCSEs either. I was young and naive really.

Then I went into HMP P------- and a YOI for a violent offence. Had a fight after a house party with my older brother's mate. Well, he got into a fight and I defended him; ended up with a three and a half year prison sentence. Started mixing with the wrong people. Stopped playing football completely. Played five-a-side rarely. Didn't have the drive; I was with different people. I had different stresses. I didn't have money.

After that I was out for two years and that's when I [was] caught on my first drugs charge. I got four years eight months for two ounces of cocaine and half a kilo of weed. But that sentence was when I started to change my mindset. I know I'm back here now on another sentence, but I'm telling you the truth: that was when I started to change my mindset. I knew I always had something, but I never had that opportunity to show what I had to offer. You try to give up the lifestyle but that's all I knew. It's good money, so you just do it, but you're arguing against yourself half the time.

I started playing again when I came here but then I broke my ankle against a good team in the Welsh league. I was only here for nine or ten months and I was out of action for four! Had my town visits on a Saturday, but my missus didn't drive, so I could only have them on a Saturday. So I stopped playing.

Met my missus when I was a kid, but we split up when I went to prison when I was seventeen and she was in college. I was just a kid and I couldn't expect someone to wait a year and a half at that age. We lost contact then when I got out. I bumped into her after six months. We rekindled our relationship. We've been together ever since. We've got a boy now who's my main motivation now. He was born three months prior to my previous sentence.

I started playing again for two years up until I got arrested. I was supposed to go and turn up for pre-season training for a really good team to see if I could play for them, but I ended up coming in here. Ended up being out for four years.

I didn't go straight back into drug dealing. A mate of mine had a good job as a subcontractor. He was doing alright and he got me a job with him as his mate. But after a while that didn't work out so that's when I started to dip my toe into dealing drugs, what I'm in for now. I never had a passion for it and although I did look for jobs it didn't work out. It's not something that I wanted to do, but you've got to do stuff you don't want to do if you work. I knew people from football who were trying to get me on the railways. I nearly got a job with the council; I was meeting the right people, but it just didn't work out.

It got to the point where I didn't need to do it for the money; it was a way of life. I needed money, but not thousands of pounds. I needed employment. I was trying to find what was right for me. I fully believe this time that I have come into jail for a reason. The sentences they give out, if I carried on, I could be doing ten or twelve years, where you have to say goodbye to your partner. I was caught for a reason. I'm actually happy I got caught. Had I have carried on, would I have been given a bigger sentence? Would I have been roped into a bigger conspiracy? The answer is, I believe so, yes. This time I know I won't be back in prison. I could never say that before.

Looking back, I realise I wasn't fully there; that's when I started to think a bit more about my future. I wasn't naive so I started to explore other opportunities. That's why I was out for nearly five years. I know it sounds bad, but I wasn't your average dealer, I was a family man. I was around police officers, around people you wouldn't think I would be around, and they didn't have a clue what I was doing. I used to speak to police officers about football, not as friends but as associates. I was leading a normal life, but not necessarily a law-abiding life. It was simply the life I was leading. From what I've seen I don't think they had a clue what I was doing. I was around a lot of normal people. I was away from the hustle and bustle. I did it in a smart way.

But now the difference is the green light is on. It's got to the point where my missus says I'm like a different person. Don't get me wrong; she loves me for me, but even my mates have said, "What's going on with John?" They say it's like they're speaking to someone else.

When I was playing in C------ on the six-a-side pitch, I was getting on with everyone, even the prison officers. I know it sounds bad, but they were the people I was around on the outside. I wasn't around the dealers, the bullshit, I was around normal people. I was ready to get a job, change my life. Speaking to my mate who ran a barber's and who used to do what I did, he explained how he took his opportunity, opened up the barbershop and never looked back. He's never done anything since. I knew I had to try. It didn't make sense to me how my boy is playing football and I'm in prison. That's when the lightbulb moment happened.

I knew a bit about Prescoed before I came here. There were always people who said they'd been here and they had good footballers who win the league. I knew the standard wasn't that good, but that doesn't matter. Football is enjoyable; you just want to play. So it doesn't matter about the standard, or who you're up against, you just want to play. I'd play all day every day, any weather, pitch, footwear, whatever; it's my best thing. That's why I want to go into football when I'm out. Even if I could go back, get rid of the criminal records, I'd go to university and study, that's what I would want to do. I would have liked to have worked for a football club, do my coaching badges, worked with the academies and the good youngsters. That's my passion.

The boys here know I'm a half decent player. My role in the prison is like a mentor; I support people through OMU, banking applications, housing applications, general queries, how do I do this or that, people might ask you to write a letter for them. So I've just got to make myself approachable at all times, whether it's the football pitch or normal life because of what I'm doing on camp. I think that's why I'm captain and that's recognised by staff because I've sort of got the respect of the officers to a certain degree. I was captain on the out too, so I'm used to being captain.

It's important for me. You want stability and you want to make sure you stay in open conditions. If you mess up it's going to be your own fault because they're not going to get rid of you for no reason. I was here last time, but more naive and I didn't get shipped out then, so I know I'm not going to get shipped out now. I like helping people any way I can, whether I like them or not, whether they be a sex offender, dealer, I can't turn it off. I've got to do what I was asked to do in here.

I don't demand respect, I just get respect. I don't know if it's the way I carry myself, the way I look, I don't know. Some people are sceptical at first but then they realise because I try to be a likeable person. I like to meet people and see what's on offer and look for opportunities. I go looking to the people that can provide them. I'm not going out of prison yet so I want to keep this frame of mind here. I want to get out there and take every opportunity on offer.

On a football team you've got to have communication skills, motivation skills, plus leadership skills as captain. Don't get me wrong, I take it over the top sometimes. We're not in the Premier League, but I'll scream as if we are. It can be a bit over the top sometimes, but that's just me, I'm over the top. We could be ten nil and I'd still demand more. Sometimes it's in you and I'll be like that in training. Me and Paul argue in training; we're similar like that. It could be over nothing, but you just want to win and you want to play well. After a match, I analyse my own performance in my head. That's how my mind works after the game and even during it sometimes.

When I'm on the pitch, I'm not in prison. I'm at home. That's like a town visit for me. It's an escape. This is what I would be doing on the outside. Saturday is football, for me, my missus and my son. We'd go to his game in the morning, mine in the afternoon, then Sunday playing for a different team.

I just love it. I love knowing we've got a game, going through the woods to the pitch, getting on the pitch, going up against other players. I know that you can't see the camp from the pitch, you're surrounded by woodland and hills, but I don't see it that. I'm football oriented so I don't see my surroundings.

Sometimes I bite back. It's the adrenaline because when I'm on the pitch, I'm too competitive for my own good. You should have seen me in the changing rooms after we lost a game. I felt like we'd lost the FA Cup final! They let me get it out of my system and five minutes later I was back to normal again. It was like the pressure had been released. That's just passion. You shouldn't be like that over a game, but I can't help that. It's in there. I can't get that out. That's just who I am.

I just turn into a different John when I'm on the pitch. I'm just focused; let me do what I need to do. I'm not thinking about anything else, so I'm unaware of what's going on in my mind. I'm not thinking about town visit, I'm on the pitch now, I come into my own. I thought everyone was like that, but I've discovered they're not. I don't think about anything else. I could have had a bad day yesterday and I'd probably be able to blank it out on the pitch. For that ninety minutes it's a different word.

Football motivates me like that and I want to go in to do something with the game. The John I was when I wasn't playing was far more miserable. I was no good, going out partying, doing stuff that didn't mean anything. Even when I was out doing what I was doing I was spending the majority of time with my son. He was playing football and my partner was coming along. That's now part of her life too and she's carried that on whilst I've been in here, all credit to her. But my son, he's lost his motivation a bit, which he will because I'm in here. He's dropped out of the academy now, he's in the advanced centre, but he's still playing, so he's just below the academy. He didn't get a contract in the summer. I'm not there to push him.

Not everyone in the team is from the same background. Some are from England, some are from Wales. Different offences, too; some in for stuff we might not agree with, but on the pitch, everyone is friends. There's a lot of individuals I would say, so sometimes it's not quite a team. There are six or seven who have the team ethic, then two or three who are more for themselves.

The PEO staff here are older, and they are the go-to people for us, a bit like a father figure. You'd never see them get disrespected in the same way that other staff might get it sometimes. They are fairer because they are on our level and non-judgemental. They are always polite and respectful to me and I've never ever had an issue with them. They understand certain things people may have done for whichever reasons, though they don't condone it, and this helps them relate to people here. I know some of them have been in the army. Some people don't believe how similar other people can be. We're all human.

I've seen people in the team speaking off the pitch, about football on the Saturday, getting excited, talking about the formation or who we are playing. They might communicate off the pitch, but I don't think everyone spends that much time with each other. Some are out working, some are on home leave, some are on town leave and some are at work in the prison. In the evenings I'm doing my uni work so I'll go to my cell, but some will watch a film and some go to social. In the hall, if I see someone who plays, I'll chat with them. So seeing people around, it helps to build a sense of community. A lot of the players come to me and ask if they are playing Saturday. I probably see more of the team than they do being on camp. We see each other throughout the week, so there's no arguments, no one dislikes each other.

Football in here has helped me, but that's mainly to do with my son. When he does well, it does help. That was one of the main reasons that I wanted to stop what I was doing because he was doing so well. I wanted to stop anyway, but I should have pushed it a bit more. I want to be there for him because he's doing something I love. But he could be doing piano lessons, I'd still be the same, I'd have the same mind set. Everyone wants to be proud of their children and be there. It's not just because it's football. It could be swimming, boxing, whatever he wanted to do. He deserves it. He's not a bad kid.

If there was no football here, I'd probably be the same but I'd wait to get out to play. I'd use the gym, do other sporting activities like cricket, but football's my main one. Me and Paul, we play badminton in the hall. Whatever sport it is, I'll play.

Football's helped me in here and it adds to my rehabilitation. I want to go into that kind of work; it's one of the reasons why I'm driven. It can provide motivation to people wanting to stay here and not mess around on camp. It's the same as when I'm out on that pitch, without the bite, I want to use it as a career path. I think I'm going to be successful. I don't know for sure, but I'd like to think I've got something to offer if I'm going to be given an opportunity. For sure, I want to take it. You'll see.

Daniel

Everything is here for me now: work, see family, play football. The three things I love.

Midfielder
Kitchen Orderly

I'm twenty-seven years old, served eighteen months in prison and I've got fourteen months left. This is my second sentence and I'm in for conspiracy to supply class A drugs. Before that I was in the army for six years. When I came out I struggled to get work. I couldn't get employment due to my mental health conditions from the army. Got two kids and the only way I could provide for them was to sell drugs.

First sentence was a suspended sentence, community service. I was on remand for six months and got a suspended sentence for two years. I played football straight away. I was selling drugs to most of the football team, that's the problem. They were my main clients. But if it wasn't me it would have been someone else. I know that's a bad way of looking at it, but I'll never do it again in my life.

I was a soldier in the Army and served in Germany, when I was seventeen and eighteen, then Afghanistan for four years before I went back home to the UK. Got PTSD [Post Traumatic Stress Disorder] triggered in Afghanistan. I got blown up three times. Gave me memory loss, anger, other signs. I had to have treatment for it for nine months and it came to the point where I had to leave the army. I was gutted, but they made me leave. It wasn't a discussion; it was medical discharge. They said I was a liability and I needed to get out. There was no easy or nice way of saying it.

Made me feel shit, really bad, making me out to be a liability. I wasn't allowed to carry rifles or carry out certain duties because of the meds they gave me. When you have PTSD, they treat you, but they also feed you loads of meds to try and sort you out. That messes you up even more.

I played football in the army for the regiment team, but you start off playing football against all the other squadrons in your regiment. There were fifty to sixty regiments so our regiment would play against their regiment or our squadron against their squadron. I went for trials then to go for the Royal Logistics Core (RLC) where we played against the artillery and the paras. It's much better if you're a tracksuit soldier when you reach the Core. I was a PTI [Physical Training Instructor] anyway, so I was working in the gym. I'd go training on a Wednesday and a Thursday, then Friday would be the game. We'd play Core games then every Friday to have Saturday and Sunday off. Back in work Monday.

Tracksuit solder means you're in tracksuits rather than your army gear. It's a brilliant life because it feels like you're just playing sport. If you are into anything, rugby or boxing, say, and you can make it, then you're classed as a tracksuit soldier. Training for nine months of the year then work for three; it's good. I went to trials with the regiment and when you go to a normal local team there's usually twenty to thirty players for pre-season. But in the army there's hundreds and you've got to shine to get picked out.

When they whittled it down, it was down to if your face fitted or who you knew, to be honest. Although I didn't know anyone in the Core team, I was [the] best in my regiment. My Sergeant Major was mates with someone who played and asked if one of his boys [could] come training with the Core team. Normally, the boys that played for the team are like my mates here at Prescoed in the football team. But I went down for trials and there was a hundred people all doing fitness, ball control, shooting, you name it. I did alright and they asked me to come back so I was in the first team all the way through then for the season.

Before here I was in S------ for sixteen months playing on their five-a-side pitch. It's was good for ball control, but it's five-a-side football, so not so good for much else really. In the summer, you can play more. I was a Gym Orderly, so I could play four times a week, Monday to Thursday. You don't do it Friday because that's induction day and the weekends you don't play at all.

There weren't many quality players there, just a couple. But that's how I knew of the guys here like Paul and Alan. I knew there was a football team here too because a few of my mates had played for them. Then Paul came up before me, who I'd played with, plus we were both gym orderlies. We'd both play Monday to Thursday. When he got into the team he was writing to me, saying he'd put my name forward for training so I got me straight in the team.

Although I had that connection, my main thing was just to get here and get my home leaves and town visits. The football was a bonus for me. I didn't want to come here just to play football. Don't get me wrong, I was looking forward to playing, but I hadn't put boots on for sixteen, seventeen months.

I struggled in the first training session and my first game. Getting back used to putting boots on and running around. Before, I was just banged up and you don't get time to do fitness, never mind keep on top of your fitness. But it's brilliant now and [I'm] loving it. It's helping my mental health and everything. Not just the fitness, the happiness that comes from it. I'm back doing what I love. Football was my life growing up as a kid, in the army, leaving the army, every training day, matches on a Saturday.

For that hour and a half, I just feel amazing. You forget about everything else that's happening in the world. When I'm in my bed, I'm constantly thinking about other things. Friday night I'm thinking about football, thinking about the game. Come Saturday morning I'm thinking about football, preparing for football. All that time before, and when

I've finished playing, it takes my mind off all my bad thoughts, the banging noises I have that causes me to have the shakes, anxiety and the depression. It takes all that out. I concentrate on football because it's something I love. My main thing now is I've got to get my fitness because it helps with my mental health. I don't know why or how but it's scientifically proven, and the doctors are telling me to do fitness because it will help.

At the moment I'm on sertraline, an anti-depressant, and mirtazapine, a sleeping tablet and anti-depressant. I'm doing other treatment too for my mental health, finger movements [EMDR: Eye Movement Desensitization and Reprocessing therapy]; it's something I started in the army but didn't have enough time to finish the treatment off, which is why I am what I am. In the next few months I want to come off everything and not rely on my meds all the time. I need to get out and be a normal person.

I've been a bit down in prison. In S------, I was really low because I split up with my partner. So it's helping me control my emotions a lot. Instead of thinking why am I not with her I'm thinking about football and can't wait to do this and do that. It's helping me mentally, physically, and I'm happier knowing there's a game Saturday and knowing I'm going to train on Tuesdays.

The location of the pitch here plays a part. Knowing that you're trusted to leave the jail, but it doesn't feel like a jail up here anyway. The atmosphere, everything about it, going to football, knowing we're going outside, is good. Playing outside teams, that they trust us to play against them, and the effort that everyone has gone to make a team happen.

Trust. It's massive deal for me. I left the army knowing I wasn't trusted there. Knowing someone trusts me now is important. I've got massive trust issues with everything. They say never trust a prisoner. When you've been locked up for sixteen months and they're opening the door, closing the door, doing the food, everything like that they do for you. But coming up here now, I know I'm getting that trust back with people. I can ask people stuff. I can talk to people. Trust is good.

In closed conditions everything is kind of done for you. In open, it's up to you, so you've got to do everything, which I think is amazing. But they trust us to get it done, and if you need help, you go and ask someone, that's how it is.

I haven't got to know people that close on the football team yet. I speak to them, have a laugh, [but] I don't know their personal lives or what they've gone through. I'm quite a private person.

The first ten days I was here it was horrible. I understand why people want to go back. It's because in bang up everything is routine. 8am you get up, get your breakfast, then twenty minutes for a phone call, come back at eleven, you get food, banged up till half one, you go to work, you come back at 4pm, you get food, you're banged up. That's how it was. You just know what you were doing, and you never had that free time to do anything else. The first ten days here, you do your induction, but it's only an hour a day.

Once that's done you've got the day to yourself, and you're thinking to yourself about what to do. I'm used to sitting in my room chilling out watching telly, but it's completely different down here. It was a struggle just from boredom. I knew I needed to get into a routine. Now I'm in the kitchen and my routine is brilliant. That's one main thing I need in life, a routine. Even on the out.

It's like the army. I've been in places like this on exercises, but this place is a lot better! I think this used to be an old army barracks in fact. It's just the same, get up, go down the scoff house, have your food, exactly the same as an army barracks. In the army I'd wake up at eight, go to the gym, take lessons until twelve, go to scoff house like here at twelve, have food till one, then I'm back in work at half one. Take more sessions till four or five o'clock. But here I have to stay until half six to serve the food and then I come back half six, so the day is mine to do what I want. If I want to go to the gym or play badminton, I can, plus the football on Tuesdays and Saturdays. It's exactly the same as being in the army. That's why I need that routine because then I know it will just fly by.

I have a visit on a Sunday, so I can play football on Saturday. I then work the rest of the week, but I have time off on a Tuesday for football training. My whole week is planned out now.

Everything is here for me now: work, see family, play football. The three things I love. It helps me with working as a team, socialising with people, something I don't do much because I'm a private person, and meeting new people. I used to do it all the time before I joined the army, socialising. But when I left, that's when I became a private person. I was polite, courteous, use my manners, say please and thank you, but I had a tight knit of friends and I wouldn't let anyone else in.

It's good though, they're all welcoming, the boys here. I was the new lad five weeks ago. I had a bit of pressure, especially with Paul bigging me up. I was a bit nervous for my first training session, but they all welcomed me in. I had a terrible game, I knew myself, and they said don't worry about it, as soon as your fitness comes up you'll be fine. You'd think in jail, and you're with loads of lads that play football and people are bigging you up, that they'd give you shit. That was my biggest fear, but they were welcoming. I was surprised and it made me relax.

I haven't really got to know people yet. I know them on the pitch, or when we go training, but around camp there's a couple of boys I knew. They have progressed in football, the same as me. They may not have a good first game, but by the second and third they've stepped it up a notch. I've told them not to worry about it because I was the same when I started. Couple of games later they got their touch back and were straight into it.

Eight weeks is a long time in this jail. Eight weeks in closed, you're a no one. You're still banged up, finding your feet, no job. Eight weeks here, it's a small camp; I feel like I can say hi to everyone. Near enough everyone, you see them in the gym, in the kitchen or on the servery. You see everyone come through. You talk to them there or playing football or badminton. I'm getting to know a lot more people like that.

I'm in the kitchens now, chopping veg. Paul is in there and my brother too. Both of us on the veg. It's good to have a routine. It helps having him here and he was in the army. I'm able to talk to him if I'm feeling bad. Working on the servery has been useful. Just being able to stand up, look someone in the eye, and ask them if they're alright. Ask them what they're on, have a general chat.

I hope to play when I get back out, if all goes well with my partner, but if not I'll go back to where I'm from. I'll see what my fitness is like. I don't know if I'm going to come out unfit or fit. I'll decide in my last 6 months which way I'll go, like if I want to start bulking up in the gym or if I want to stay as I am, then continue being fit, so I can play football. I'll see closer to the time. I want to go for trials for a club where a couple of my mates play.

When I was in S------, I come in at ten stone and I'm thirteen stone now. I'm trying to get in a nice shape and I'm trying to put weight on. I'm comfortable where I am now. I'm small and when I think things like that, it gets in my head. I just want to train, train, train, to get bigger and bigger, because I want to be in a nice comfortable body for when I get out. My last three to six months, I don't know what's going to happen.

If there hadn't been a footy team here I think it would be boring. It's lucky that I love football and that is my life, even on the outside. Any spare time I'll play with my little boy, training him to be a footballer. If there wasn't football here I'd have a visit Saturday, bored Sunday, Tuesday I'd just be playing badminton. Something I'm good at, but I don't enjoy it. There's only so much badminton you can play!

When I get out, I'd want to get a house near my kids on release. I've got to be there otherwise I'll be a weekend dad then, something I do not want. I never had a dad; it's just my mum at home. So for my boy, that's what I want to do, be there for every game, every training session, take him anywhere he needs to be. Take days off work if I need to. He might change his mind as he grows up, but as it stands, he wants to play football.

I've never had a dad to come and support me playing football. My uncle acted like a father to me, plus my cousin came to every single game that I played, and then they both came to watch me play in the army. When I left they came and watched me play, wherever I played.

I think back to when I played at a high level, semi-pro. That was when I was in the army, going through my treatment, and we're getting forty pound a game. I could have played higher, Welsh Premier maybe, because I was training with a team all the time, but I never got to sign. I had a bad gambling addiction so I had to make money. If I was getting paid to play football, would it have made me more stable? Maybe not at the time, but now? Yes, I think so.

Where I am now, eight weeks in here, compared to in a year's time, things might be different. I'll nearly be out. Twelve months is a long time. I'm going to be out working, soon so who knows where I'm going to be by then.

Jermaine

You play the game or ruin it all for yourself.

Forward

I've been at Prescoed for around 10 months now. I've been in custody for 2 years, for drug offences, but I'm working now and I'm due to come out next year just in time for Christmas. I'm hoping to work all the way through till then. They'll give me two weeks off over Christmas then straight back in to work.

It's my fifth time in prison and my last. First went in when I was fifteen when me and my mates broke into a warehouse. It was a storage company, so I got arrested for burglary, and they sent me to a YOI. The second one was dangerous driving, the third was ABH after I got in a fight in the town centre, the fourth was a recall for that, but this was my long one, six years. I'm twenty-six now and I came in when I was twenty-three.

Every time I've been inside, I've always gone to the gym and trained and played football. I've always played for teams, like the wing team, and every prison I've been to I've played on teams against officers or other wings. I've always been involved in all that. They do other things as well in some prisons like boxing, basketball and touch rugby. I played a lot of rugby when I was there, but football is me through and through. Supported Man United, but I've changed to City now.

I've been inside A-------, G---------, B--------, P---, C------, and Prescoed. Played in all of them. This one has been the most useful to me. I've had the opportunity to come up here because where I come from people don't tend to change their life; they stay in the same cycle. I've never really known any different. I've never had a job or even thought about getting a job. I've always seen the easy way to make money. Now I've come up here and I've seen a different perspective. They've rehabilitated me to go out to work. I've landed myself a job and I'm quite happy with it. I like coming back at the end of the day having a cup of tea and jumping into bed. I feel ancient. Even my knees hurt after a game on the weekend!

It's my first time in Prescoed and I heard about it before I came. They played on a full-size pitch and they play outside teams and they're in a league. So I was intrigued to put my skills to the test. When I first came, last season was just ending. After I did my induction, and I think there were two games left in the season, I couldn't get in the team for the first game, as they had their players already. But the second game, they needed players, so I came on as a sub. I've scored loads of goals, including on my debut.

It was hard to get used to at first. I hadn't played on a full-sized pitch or grass for so long. But with time and dedication, training every Tuesday, you get used to it. In fact, if there's an opportunity to play football I'm not going to miss it. I'll go even if I've got a broken toe! Every Tuesday was like a religion to me. Football comes first and for me it has made a difference. It is doing something productive with your time. You can only go to the gym so many times without getting bored, but you can never get bored of playing football. You have your ups and downs, some days you play good, some days you play bad. It's the thrill of the game and it's exercise at the end of the day.

I still go to the gym every day, but when I play football it's more like a team game, not just you and the gym. You've got to think three steps ahead when you're playing. You've got to work it out for yourself. It's a mind game. You've got to have a football brain.

It's given me peace of mind. I've always played football, even when I was younger, at quite a high level. When I haven't been in prison, I don't play. I might go and have a kick about with the boys, but I don't play for a regular team unless someone phones me and says, "Do you want to play a game on the weekend?" I wouldn't go out my way to play for a team. I've changed my life a bit. When I get out, I might get involved a bit, but only if I can get fitter than I am. I've got to give up the vapes first!

I've seen the team change in my time here, the whole team. It was me at first, then Neil came here a week after me. He was sub at that first game. That team has changed. They've all gone, from the keeper all the way up.

With some people coming into the team, it has helped them, it's brought their confidence out. There's a couple you see, you speak to them on the camp, [but] when they play football you see a different side to them because they're more confident. Some are a bit like me and they have a shy side. So I say to them, "You ok? I'm alright." That's it. But then on the football pitch they're telling you what to do. It's like the pitch is their natural environment, when they feel the ball at their feet, and prison is unnatural.

When I started I thought I was going to be amazing. I had come from playing in closed conditions and I was good on the five-a-side pitch. A couple of the boys I knew who were up here asked me if I still played football. I said, "Yeah. Wait until you see me on the pitch." I thought I'd look good, but I was terrible. They put me in midfield and I was absolutely shit! But then I got my chance when they put me up front and I scored six! I've been banging them home ever since. I think I'm on fifty-two so far this season.

When you're playing, it takes your mind off prison. You don't think about where you are, but some teams will mouth off to us telling us to go back to our cell! There's one geezer in one team, he's done it for years, chopsing off at us. He's never won but still comes up. I tell him, "Look at the score mate; you're nineteen nil down!" Whereas before I'd be squaring up to him and be wanting a fight. But up here you can't do that anymore, so you learn to handle it a bit better.

Beside the football, I spend my time just going to the gym; that's my main focus. It helps me get a release, release my stress. Times do get hard, and you do think that it's not you serving a sentence, it's your family. You've got it good here you know: two meals a day, going to work, no bills. I was living with my missus, we had a house, we were breeding dogs and had a nice car; everything we wanted. When I got arrested, they took all that away. Car, dogs, missus's car. It's a kick in the teeth. I feel bad then because she's had to go back home and live with her mum. I'm working hard so we can get some more money together to get a house when I'm out. She's stood by me every day. She's a good girl, never missed a phone call or a visit. She is really good. She's always saying to me that she doesn't know how I've done it. And I said, I dunno how you've done it either, but we have.

She was up here for family day recently and she comes up every family day, every visit. It was good, but I got a bit stressed out by it all. Everyone was trying to show off, me included. I wanted to do better. But I scored two, so it's not bad.

If there hadn't been football here, it wouldn't have made too much difference to me really. From the day I got sentenced, I said to my missus that I wanted to make it as easy as I could for her. I wanted to get my enhanced, I wasn't going to mess about. My plan was always to get up here and have more visits. I had to work towards getting here, and by luck I had an early review. I had over five years, but they did my review after six months and I got it three months early. I came up here with about thirteen or fourteen months in closed conditions. I'm now halfway and I've kept my word. She said she won't walk away so long as I don't give her a reason to. I haven't and she's stuck by me. It's a two-way thing.

I go out now every two weeks for town visits and I get home leave in eight weeks. I can't wait. Five days I get, straight out. She's looking forward to it as well.

In terms of playing football and reoffending, you make your own choices. You're not going to go out and think, "I want to play football, so I'm not going to sell this bag to so and so, or not make this money because I want to play football tomorrow. Or I'm not going to get into a fight with this guy because I want to play football tomorrow when he made me look like a twat." In those times you forget about the football. You don't think like that. When you are playing football you just think, "Right. I'm playing now", and everything else is left out there, that this is my time to play.

But up here, football plays its part. If someone left the weights out in the gym, just one person, if someone don't come and put the weights away, the staff say, "We're banning the gym and banning football", then the whole jail would be there to make sure that doesn't happen. It's a good thing to do. It's about having respect. They've taken the time to take you out, even if it's raining, to play football. So you have to show respect back. The gym staff are firm, they'll shut the gym, but they're fair. They have got a bit more respect in that way, maybe because they've got something people want. They're all nice geezers anyway. They've been working in prisons for thirty-odd years some of them. Some officers have never worked in a jail; they've come straight to D Cat. If they spoke to people in closed conditions like they speak to us up here, I don't think they'd be there very long.

Here, you've [got] more to lose here so you'll bite your tongue. Some will say they don't care about D Cat, do whatever you've got to do. You play the game, don't you? You play the game or ruin it all for yourself.

Joe

The way I spoke to you, you would have never have known I was in prison… That's because of football.

Forward
Transport Orderly

I've been in prison for fifteen years now. My sentence is joint enterprise, murder. I've not got a violent side to me. I've not been in trouble in my sentence and to do fifteen and a half years not having a fight or anything is probably unheard of. I'm not that type of person. I'm friendly, but I'm fair and I don't really get involved in trouble, you know what I mean?

I've been around different prisons and I've taken part in different teams throughout my prison sentence. I was involved in sport when I was a kid but I never really played what I'd call competitive sports. I just used to play with my friends for fun. But then I've come to prison and started playing with different teams. I've got just under three years left to serve hopefully and then I'll be getting out. I've done different courses to do with sport and gym. I've done my gym instructor level two, a level three health and fitness, first aid at work, level two sports leader, and level three first aid at work. I'm also a spin cycle instructor and I used to take the classes in my last jail for the staff and inmates. I've even done my Community Sports Leader Awards and Duke of Edinburgh, so I've done quite a few courses really.

Played rugby in prison too. My first team one was when I was in HMYOI A-------- where I played rugby for two years. Trained on a Wednesday and we had outside teams coming in on a Saturday. All home games of course, and it was full contact. A couple of the officers played with us, but it was mainly inmates, all eighteen to twenty-one years old. We played some good teams, from the RAF, all the teams surrounding us; it was a good league and a good standard. We had a family day with the rugby, like here with the football, to tie in [with] the final of a cup competition. Unfortunately, our opposition were three or four levels higher. Somehow we beat them nineteen [to] seventeen. My mum and dad got to spend the day and watch the game, then we had a curry after and we sat down together. It was a really nice day, with my mum and dad getting to see me play.

If they had another family day here, I think it's good. My family live a distance away, but for something like that they would probably travel to see me play. At A-------- it was amazing. It was a red-hot day and I've got a picture in my cell of my mum and dad on the side in the motion of us passing the ball along to each other. They'd never been to anything like that before, so it was really nice. The other lads' families were there too, and we spent about twenty minutes with them at the start before we went and got changed. We played the game, came back in, had a shower and they set the hall up so we could sit down and have a chicken curry together. That was the first time since I'd been in prison that I'd got to spend with my mum and dad like that, rather than just visits, after about two years inside.

I left there and went to HMP K------- when I was twenty-two and I played football for the team there. It was an adult establishment, but I was there for six and a half years playing in the local Premier League on a Saturday. They had a very good team and there's also book that's about them. We had training Tuesday, Thursday, then playing on a Saturday. All the lads from the jail could come out and sit round the field and watch, so it was a good environment to play in.

After there I went to HMP G--- M----, but we didn't have a team there. We just had a seven-a-side pitch, so we just used to do tournaments in the prison, one wing against another. Soon then I came here to Prescoed and started playing for the team. In fact, I played on the first Saturday I was here. I came on the Friday and played on the Saturday; it was good.

Although I hadn't done my gym induction, they knew I'd been in jail for a long time, so they said come down and we'll sort your gym induction out later. In fact, I hadn't even been in jail in twenty-four hours because they kicked off at two and I got here at three on the Friday! I knew some of the lads, so they must have put a word in for me. I was a sub for that game and I came on for the second half. Since then I've played nearly every time there's been a game, but because of the weather fixtures have been few and far between lately. I played in goal on Saturday because the goalkeeper lasted about three seconds when he got injured.

They've got a good team, even though it varies week by week. People are in and out, on town visits, home leave. Sometimes it's just getting enough people to play. At Christmas, we could have had a game but there were so many people on home leave from the prison, it didn't leave many to play football. It's a good set up here. The games are competitive and the pitch is nice.

I used to fix the equipment at Guys Marsh. I was there for four years, so me and a colleague would take all the equipment apart and maintain it and then it would get a full service. We used to order all the stuff, get it in, refurbish and re-do all the equipment. Then when it was inspected, they could tick everything off and say it's fine. I said to the gym officer here you need to have someone maintaining it because they don't spray the bars, the metal with oil to protect it from rust, so some things don't move properly up and down the guides. Then it bends the plastic and it breaks, because the cables are stripped of the outer coating, and it's on the metal, it's not very good.

I think a couple of the lads I'd met before in other prisons [who] had been here or got sent back on other sentences had said there was a team. I don't think it's documented in the prisoner's handbook though. They say they've got a pitch here, but it doesn't mention the football team. A lot of jails need to have a package of what they offer. The gym here is very under par. The equipment is knackered and there's no money spent on the gym here. It's the poorest gym I've been in. Don't get me wrong, the football pitch is amazing, but the gym equipment is not very good.

I've got a long lie down period, thirteen months. My escorted visits start in July this year and unescorted next April. That's the way it is because of the time I came here with. Obviously, I've been well behaved. I've got three years left in jail, which is the maximum time you can come to a D Cat as a lifer.

Being here, it's good and it's made a difference to me. Straight away I started meeting the lads who play football because they know everybody here and they've been here a while. By meeting them you get to meet everyone else quicker, so you settle down easier. Once you start walking past people and saying hello to people other people see that and think, "Oh right, okay". It's just the way jail works. I was lucky I knew a few people here anyway, but even more so because I've spoken to the football lads, got straight on the team, and got playing. Even if I hadn't got on the team I would have gone to training anyway. The only reason I play sport is for fitness; I like to stay fit. I do a bit of running and that. It's nice to stay fit. Football is a bit of variation in what you're doing.

I loved the rugby too though, but I never played it before in my life. When I went to Aylesbury I started in the football team first. Then my friend, another lifer, said, "Why don't you come and play rugby?" At first I said I didn't fancy it because I'd never played before and I thought I'd be crap. But he encouraged me to just come and try it. I just took to it like a duck to water.

At first I was a hooker and then I played fly-half. When they looked at me they thought I wasn't going to be very quick. I was quite fat but I was growing up and I was lightning fast, even though I was big. I've got a massive kick on me, and after I'd been hooker for a bit, the fly-half left, so I asked and they said they would try me there. I was banging them through the post and they were happy. Scored a few tries but most of the points I scored were from kicks. In the one semi-final we played in the whole game was nil-nil at full-time. Then we had extra time and it was still nil-nil. But in the ninety-eighth minute we had a penalty on the half-way line. I said I wanted to take it even though it was fifty metres to the posts. I hit it straight through the middle and we won after a hundred minutes of rugby.

I remember that game so well. I was dead on my feet and everything went in slow motion because I was so tired. The whole game had been tackle after tackle after tackle, but nobody had scored a try, which was unusual because someone always scored. I remember that cold feeling where everything slows down. That's what that felt like. I had the penalty, and I thought I'm going to hit it and it just went straight through and we won three-nil. The relief was more than anything! We kicked off, we took it and then just held it for a minute until we booted it out on the final whistle to win.

Most good things in jail have happened around sport for me. Within the establishment they put emphasis in a lot of places on sport because it helps take the aggression away. With rugby, the lads are very testosterone fuelled, but they are very disciplined too. You might have a fight on the rugby pitch, but then you shake hands at the end. Players pound away at each other for eighty minutes, so if you have got any aggression it's taken away. I'm surprised more jails don't do it. There are a few lads who before they played rugby were quite aggressive, but then when they played they took on the mentality of the team and they calmed down because all their energy is being used in that eighty minutes. We're talking twenty to thirty-year olds who were up to eighteen stone and were not small. It's a lot of aggression, but it's controlled.

At the end of the day when they blow the whistle you come in. When they're saying something, you stand still and you listen because if you don't, you get a round of fucks put into you, or you do a hundred burpees on the spot, or you're going back to the wing. That's just how it was. A lot of the PEOs, they're all massive and they don't take no shit. You start messing about they'll either beast you to within an inch of your life or they'll just get rid of you. It's as simple as that.

In prison, sport can have a massive influence on the lads. When they first come in, they might not have any friends. But then they come to training, become friends with people, and it's a good way to get involved in the prison social circle. You don't have many friends in prison. If you're coming to football or rugby training and you're on the wing and you see me, you might say hello and I'll say hello back. Whereas before you might not have said anything because you didn't know me, but you've got that bond. Like when you play for the team, there's that side of it. It's not just for the people who play. When I was in Kingston, all the lads on Saturday, who didn't play football but watched, talked about it on Saturday, couldn't wait to get out and watch. Plus the hype, looking at the team sheet even though they weren't on the team, little side bets going on. It's good camaraderie. Everyone knows on a Saturday the Arrows are playing; there would be a good vibe about the jail. When it's cancelled it brings the whole mood down. So it can have a broader influence on the life of the jail as well.

When football gets cancelled because of the weather, obviously, it's good for the weight trainers because they get an extra day of weights, but then it's swings and roundabouts. Saturday when the football's on, there's no weights for the jail because of the way the gym runs, so the weight trainers, they are not happy about that. But everyone else, a lot of the lads if they're not off camp, they're pissed off because they can't train. But for me, I've not experienced the outside world yet, so I'm just happy being on camp. The environment here is still good for me, but when the football isn't on, they're moping about and bored, so it does have an effect on people's mood.

For me, coming here to an open prison, it's pretty much like a duck to water, because obviously D Cat is what I've always wanted. It's always been the end goal before release, so for me I was happy to get here as soon as I can. Some people said I wouldn't like it, but whether I'm here or on the wing, I can be out until half eight or ten at night in the social room, or someone can sit in your room if your back on the wing until twelve. For me there's a lot of benefits to being in this jail. You're not bothered by other people. If you want to go outside you can. If you want to go walk around you can. If you want to go sit on a bench or the grass you can. Whereas in closed conditions you're told when you're going out and when you're going in, so there's all that to contend with. Here, it's like a breath of fresh air. I've been here since November and already It's the middle of January. It's really good; times flying.

I wouldn't call this place a prison. It's not. A prison is fences, barbed wire. That's what you're used to. It's nice to just look around and see sheep and fields and cars going along the road. Knowing that the trust is there, the freedom is there. For me, when I first walked out onto the pitch for the first time, just walking through the woods is amazing, but when I walked out, I imagined what it would feel like to walk out onto Real Madrid or Old Trafford. You just had that feeling of occasion. It was nice. In my head I thought, wow! It just takes you back. It was my second day here and I got to walk through the forest and then see two football fields. All that was really nice. There is a sense of freedom then because you are away from the jail. It's only five minutes' walk, but it does feel a bit like you are away from prison.

It's a nature walk really. I've done a few of the over fifties walks even though I'm not over fifty. They walk up the fields, through the farm and all through the woods. I've been about four or five times and I'm the only one who turns up. It's mad! I can't understand it. Walking up there, you've got a forest, a brook with water flowing by you, a bridge, badger sets, and it's lovely. It's a different world to what everyone is used to being in closed conditions.

When I was a kid, I was always outside. School summer holidays I'd be out from eight in the morning to ten at night, climbing trees and playing out. I used to wear camouflage and we'd have two teams where you'd hide and they'd try to find you and take you back to their post. I lived in a cul-de-sac in a small village where there was just me, my brother, my neighbour and another lad down the road. We just used to play together with a few other people around the estate. We were always out playing football. World Cup up the field, two jumpers, two trees. So when you walk through the trees, where I lived, it's like this. The smells, the noises. It's like walking through the forest back home for me and I spent a lot of time there growing up.

The football is important to me here because it's one of a number of new things I'm trying every week here. There's so much more I've got to come, town visits, home leave, so after being in jail for such a long time that's something you really look forward to. The football in some ways helps you to get you to that next point. It's a good stop gap for the next part of my sentence because sometimes there will be times when I'm at work or on town visits and I won't be able to play on a Saturday. So then when I can't play, someone else will be here, and they'll have the experience.

For a lot of us playing in the team it's like a professional game to a degree out there. You have a referee and play against teams from the outside, but it would be very different if you were watching eleven Prescoed boys against another eleven Prescoed boys. It would be a completely different scenario. It would probably be more violent, more comings together. Prisoners against prisoners is always going to cause conflict.

Football and sport obviously teaches control, how to use your aggression in a controlled, proper manner. When you play sport, you need to be aggressive, you can't be weak, but it's how you use it. If you're going in for a fifty-fifty tackle you can't pull out. You need to go in one hundred percent. If you're shoulder to shoulder you need to have that extra aggression to push him off, otherwise you're the one on the floor. It teaches you how to use your aggression properly.

It's like the game at the weekend. I was in goal and their number ten, as he came in, his foot nearly caught my shin because he had his foot up. So I told him. But there's a difference between telling someone and doing something. It's a warning to say, "Listen, don't do that again, because next time I'll be coming through you!" You develop that ability around sport. But some lads can be put in that situation and they'll punch his head in. I've even seen it playing volleyball and that's not even a contact sport! But because they bumped into each other in the middle on the net they were fighting.

It's different at training though because you're not playing for anything. If there was enough people here to have a team from each unit, and there was a trophy at the end of it, you would see a difference. Trust me, I've seen it all. You play a friendly, there's no issue, maybe a murmur, but when you're playing for something, then people's competitiveness comes out and slide tackles become aggressive. It's like when you have a derby, like City against United or Chelsea against Tottenham. They go in harder because it's like they're wearing a badge of pride because it's a derby. Whereas if it were a normal game, they wouldn't. You see it all the time in professional football, that's just the way it is. It does teach you to be social; you've got to have a laugh, take some banter. In the changing rooms before, everyone's throwing things around, balls are being kicked about, people are excited to get out there, so it teaches you take things on the chin and deal with it. There's a lot of banter. A bunch of grown men in a room, there's going to be a lot going on.

If you were to look at our games from above you'd think it was just two teams playing football. That is until you come down. You hear the name of our team and the lads talk about it that know we are prisoners. If you took us to an away game and people watched us, the other team, they wouldn't know we were from a prison until they asked or talked to us. People wouldn't realise where we are from.

I don't really know if I will carry on playing when I get out. I'll be thirty-six when I'm released. I know it's not old and I'll be fit, but life's going to take over. Family, kids hopefully. I've got a fiancé, but I haven't got kids yet, but obviously it's a priority. I've also got to earn money. I've been in jail for fifteen years, so I've no savings, I was only eighteen when I started my sentence.

Don't get me wrong, if there's a five-a-side on a Monday when I'm at work or I meet someone then I would play, but as for signing up for a team, no. One, I don't think I'll be able to commit, and two, I can't be injured. If I get hurt it could take me out of work and I can't risk that. I'd like to play football, but there's that risk. I'm going to be moving to a new city, where I've never lived before, as I can't go back home because of the victim's family, so I'm going to have to start again somewhere else.
This was my first time in prison and when I get out I've got to begin again at the starting point of what an eighteen year old would do, but I'll be thirty-six. I've got to make up for eighteen years lost! I've got a lot of work to do, like get a mortgage and get a job. As soon as I'm allowed to work stage two, that's what I'll do, work as much as I'm allowed and save money. Hopefully, when I'll leave, I'll have fifteen to sixteen thousand to take with me. That's the plan.

I didn't come here for the football, I came here because it's the best D Cat to come to in a lot of ways. But if there's no football here, but you've still got the gym and badminton, I think it would be a massive downfall on the jail. Because the gym is not the best, the sports hall is about as high as this ceiling, so you've got to play a different game of badminton there. It's one court, it's not even a full court, so you can't move side to side! The football here is probably one of their main things; it's a massive bonus to this place.

There should also be a prisoner sign-up list, where lads can put their names down, and there's thirty to forty spaces where they can come on a Saturday and watch. It gets them not quite off camp, but there's plenty of space for them to come and watch because it adds a different atmosphere. When I was in Kingston the lads used to come and watch; that was B Cat. The lads are all there, no one is going to run off, you could go whenever you wanted. If you're up there or down here, you've still got the same opportunities to walk across that field any time. Maybe they should say we'll have thirty to forty lads on that list, put your name down, and we'll go over. I don't think it would be that much of a hassle for them to do. At the end of the day the boys are here anyway. There's no security checks that need to be done, the lads live on camp, the ball boys can go over, but it would be better if you could have the lads stand where there's plenty of room. Might make a difference to the atmosphere too, having supporters?

I think that lads who play football and are training are less likely to be doing drugs, so less likely to be involved in behaviours that could stop them from playing football. There are a lot of positives, especially in closed conditions. In Guys Marsh we never had teams coming in, but a couple of times we did five-a-side. We had six people from each wing, eight wings, so that's forty odd people on the Astroturf. Some of those people playing would normally be on the side spiced out [of] their nut, but for at least one day they might see a different side to life, might stop them smoking that spliff that day, might be the difference to them in making a change. There is that aspect. To be on the football team you have to be fit. If you aren't fit, you aren't going to get picked, so you have to look after yourself. It gives a benefit to you, the healthy lifestyle, the NHS with reducing obesity, so it does help in that respect. It does play a big part in the prison system as a good way of stopping reoffending, but what would be good was if the prison had links to teams from different areas. So that someone could ring them up and say, "Alright mate, we've got Joe leaving prison this week. Would you be interested in giving him a trial?" If they set up football for you when you're released, it's giving you a pathway. You might not get in, but you could do training and make friends in that team and that way you would have a bit of a social network when you get out of prison. If you get out and you've got nobody, you could easy turn back to crime or drugs. If you're going to go out and you've got training on one evening, or the local team is going to give you a chance, it might make the difference to you not reoffending again.

That is the biggest downfall in prison. The missing link between community and prison. People are too scared to have the link because they're scared of the consequences if something goes wrong. So instead of doing this and promoting it, maybe people are scared by what others may think. But at the end of the day the papers will say bad things anyway. When I was in A--------, some of the lads that were leaving, they had a mechanics garage where you did an eighteen-month course, and if you completed that course start to finish and you passed the garage would give you a job on release straight away. They had everything. New cars were in there, tools and they were taught everything. As long as you were leaving prison within a year of completing that course, they took you on.

Here, there are teams that come in every week; the prison should set up a file. The majority of people here are Welsh, so they're going to be going back into the surrounding areas. They should have links to say that this lad is coming out, he's a good footballer, and does anyone fancy giving him a trial. It would be good for them, for the prison, for reducing reoffending. Give them something to focus on, going out.
The first few months going out is going to be precarious for them. They're going to be back in their old life or circle of friends. So if they could go out and meet new people who are involved in sport, not involved in the drug scene or anything like that, it could make a difference. It might only make a difference to one person, but that's one person you're not going to have back in jail. It's a stepping stone. I know it's a risk, but there's a risk in everything that happens in prison. If you take that risk it could be golden, it could make a massive difference. Every time I've had a game with one of the outside teams I've had a chat with the lads afterwards on the side-line. They ask you how long you got left and everything. They aren't seeing an issue and their club might not have a problem either. They might be happy to have you, especially if they need an extra player or two.

At the family day recently one of the people's family members, he was speaking to me because I'd come off, and he said to me, the way I spoke to you, you would have never have known I was in prison because of the conversation we had. This lad who had never met me before said he wouldn't have known I was in jail. That was a good way to look at it. That's because of football. In sport, if you were an officer and I was an inmate that conversation wouldn't flow as it did in that arena because you still have that line. Instead, we talk on the side of the pitch just like two people at the side of any football match having a conversation.

Alan

In a team you need to pull together and that's the same in the prison.

Squad member
Kitman
Ballboy
Gym Orderly

So I'm in my late thirtles, married and got kids. I was a will writer, a funeral planner and I've also done some stocks and shares as well before jail. Played a lot of rugby, which I love, plus I do karate, and I love MMA [Mixed Martial Arts]. But then I got a sentence of four and a half years for conspiracy to supply class A drugs.

I was at S------ for just over six months before I came here. I did quite a bit of sport down there. Gym every day plus five-a-side football, badminton, indoor tennis. I then progressed and had the Gym Orderly's job, so I was doing sport every day. The Gym Orderly role was basically to come in the morning, hand out the football shirts, make sure everything was switched on, go and play football with the boys if the numbers were down, clean up after every session, four sessions a day, clean the showers, wipe the machines down. That was it day after day.

I nearly didn't come to Prescoed. When I went to prison first of all, the main aim was to get D Cat. You can have a six-month or a twelve-month review depending on your sentence. They told me they were going to give me a six-month review so that's why I stayed at my first prison because it was better for me personally to get my D Cat from there. But if I had a twelve month I was going to go to P--- which I didn't mind. That's because they have a better sports facility and they played touch rugby there, which is my main passion. But then I wanted to come here so I could work outside then and to provide for my family; that was my main focus.

I've been here fourteen weeks now, just over three months. I use the gym every day, we go to badminton, sometimes we play tennis, indoor football, skittle football, and I've joined the football team as well. I never really played football before I came to prison. I played at school like everybody does, but as soon as school finished, I never played again until I came here and that's when I started playing again.

There are aspects of playing rugby that are transferrable to football like fitness, but for me it's a different type of fitness. A different awareness around you. With rugby, you're looking in front of you and to the side; with football you've got to be aware of all around you. It made me a bit more spatially aware. If someone came from football to rugby it would be a different type of awareness again. But for me it just made me more aware of someone behind or to the side of me.

81

The team at Prescoed has a high reputation and I knew about it before I came. People have come to Prescoed, and for various reasons have had to go back to their other prisons on a recall, and their stories come back. Like how the prison haven't lost the league for so many years.

So I started playing to keep fit. Even if we haven't got a game, we're still training, and for that hour of the day you can forget everything. You're out there with your mates having a run round keeping fit. That was one of the main things for me, and making new friends. It made fitting into Prescoed a lot easier. When you come and join the team you make friends that much easier.

To get to the field you've got to walk down the steps and through the woods so you end up nowhere near the prison. You feel totally away for it for that ninety minutes and you can relax and enjoy yourself for that time.

The fact that you can't see the prison has a bit of an impact. In Prescoed, it's quite relaxed anyway. If it was an enclosed prison and you went away it would have more of an impact, but you feel like you're away from the prison so you feel like you're not inside. Getting involved makes me feel happier. It does make a difference. Also, it does help with [the] mental side of jail because you get away from everything. Even if you're having problems at home, if you go to football you forget about it. It does help. You have a laugh with your mates, with the other prisoners. And it's a different type of fitness for me, which I enjoy. In rugby, I'm a winger, so I'm mainly sprinting with a little bit of rest. It's little bursts of energy. With football, it's more of a continuous run; it's changed my fitness aspect that way.

You're working together at the end of the day. There's new people coming in all the time, it's good to accept them in, make them feel comfortable and welcome as well. In a team event, you need to pull together, and that's the same in the prison. There's less arguments; everyone is friendly with each other. Arguments are resolved through conversation.

There are convicts here, and little things in prison are massive to us. On the outside it might be minute but not in here. Things can get heated quite easily over little things on the inside because it is magnified. This is a goldfish bowl environment. Knowing the boys through football, you'd rather talk it out than have an argument.

I've seen a difference between football here in an open prison and football in a closed prison. Football in closed can get quite heated, to the point where there's almost blows exchanged every day. But up in here it's a different environment; it's relaxed, friendlier.

It's something I learned from rugby as well. You always have disagreements and arguments, but it's knowing when to walk away and when you've done wrong. Knowing when to hold your hands up and say sorry. I find that more with rugby than with football.

With rugby, it's more of a gentleman thing really. It's rougher, but you've got more respect for each other. You see it on telly too, or maybe I'm a bit biased, because I love rugby so much!

It also helps improve relations between staff and prisoners. We've got to respect them, and we try to get on with all the prison staff, the prison officers. We get on better with the gym officers. It's a different relationship.

I've seen a difference too on people who have come in and played football here. You get quite strong characters in the group, and they sort of try and run things. The younger boys come in and they just try to listen to what the older boys are saying.

I think sport can help build character, particularly in prison, because it helps build people's confidence. You can see the younger ones learning off the older ones and changing their attitude. The younger ones will come in with a bit of attitude then after a session or two they're changed. They're friendlier and they've got a lot of patience with their fellow players. Like with me as well because I've got two left feet! I try to put myself in good positions, but it often doesn't come off. Still, they've all got patience with me. I'm a lot older than the boys, most are mid-twenties, so they are a lot fitter, so when I do mess up, they don't shout at me, they just carry on playing. They see me out there playing all the time and I'm a bit older than them as well.

I'm a friendly type of guy. I don't really get into any altercations. If I mess up, I put my hands up and say sorry. Nobody has a go at me like that. I don't know if it's because I'm a bit older I get respect or whether I've been there for quite a bit of time now.

Helps that I'm a Gym Orderly too, I think. I've got a bit of respect for that. I'm also in the prison band as well. We're called Wrong Direction! We've got a concert coming up for Christmas. I'm the singer, so I just try to be friendly to everyone.

I think when I'm released I'll be going back to rugby, even back to coaching, hopefully. My old club have said I can have a position back with them, maybe even for my ROTL. I know they're in contact with the prison. I spoke to the governor about it and he said he wants more ties with the larger companies like that, so they can't see any problem with it not going through. I'll be going back to rugby. I think I have a year left in me. My son is coming up now, and he will be in youth, a year after I leave prison. That will force me to stop playing after that. I might have a few veterans' games and stuff like that, but at the moment I'm still focused on playing another year of rugby when I get out.

When my son was younger, he went to the next village over, to the school, and he wanted to start playing rugby, which was great for me. He started playing for their local team. He went there for a year then they asked me if I wanted to step in and start coaching them because I'd been doing bits and bobs with them anyway. I did my coaching badges and I've been with them ever since. That really is one of my passions, which I miss. I started coaching with them and after a while they asked me to coach the school boys. I did a year and a half coaching them and I also helped out with the rugby team which my son was involved in. I love coaching kids, seeing how they progress. There's nothing better than taking a new child that can't pass the ball and then watch them over the year and see how they develop just gives me so much joy. It's an amazing feeling. I could even use my time in here. Going around the schools talking about my experience. Steering them away from going down the wrong path and just sticking with sport.

It would definitely have made a difference to me if the football hadn't been here. I just enjoy going over there. Sometimes I don't really enjoy the football, but I enjoy going over with the boys, spending time with your mates, having a run round, getting that hour out because I can't see myself playing football when I leave! But it makes a hell of a difference for me in here. It's changed, it makes me happy in here. Football is a big part of prison life.

Does it play a part in reducing reoffending? I don't know, I honestly don't, so I can't say yes or no because it's my first time in prison. The experience I've had has been a good one with sport because it makes you feel happier. I would like to think it would, but coming to a prison for the first time, I didn't know that many criminals beforehand. I would like to think some people, before coming to prison, go down the wrong path, take drugs, they get in a vicious circle, and then they come to prison. Most of the time [when] they burgle or thieve it is to get money to take drugs. If they come and do sport in prison, join the gym, play football, and then join a team when they are released, then there's no reason for them to do drugs. So, in that respect, it kind of helps them lead a cleaner and healthier life, rather than going back to the drugs and burglary. It would help in that way because they feel better about themselves, they enjoy the team aspect of the football then in prison. Then when they go out, they join a team of some sort, then rather than taking drugs and going down the wrong path again. They could stay healthier in all areas of their life.

Chris

It's not always been easy, but I'm always a fighter and willing to prove people wrong.

Forward
Eastleigh FC

I've done a bit of time in prison and I served time at Prescoed. Since I came out I did a little bit of work on sport helping people inside. I'm now at Eastleigh FC playing, doing coaching in the community. I'm still on licence, and I did do a bit of work when I first come out, but I've eased off a bit because I've had a few challenges and struggles when I was released, but I'm looking to go back and do it again in the future. It's all the same thing, coaching and mentoring, really, isn't it? As a footballer, it's good for me and my Image by trying to build bridges.

I'm involved in doing a bit of mentoring now and I like to think it helps because of my own experience. I was also interviewed for a role with Great Expectations based in Cheltenham and Gloucester, going into different schools. They have a seven-week programme where they look for kids that are struggling in school academically, or might have some problems at home, alcohol or other problems, and they do a seven-week programme. The first week is just getting to educate kids on the law, second week is about drug dealing, alcohol and substance misuse. Third week was about joint enterprise, and so on. I only did it for three months, started mentoring kids, and eventually the governor pulled it in the end because I was driving, and he didn't know. But my offence was a driving offence! So, looking back, it gave me a taste of using my negative experience in a positive way. I got a good message across to the lads about my story. I conveyed it all to them, about what happens if you get in trouble, the crime and the certain paths you take. It's a powerful story, really. I had a good lifestyle, playing football, and then went to jail.

I'm a bit of a journeyman. I played professional football for about ten years before I went to jail. I've had struggles at times with drink and I've had problems with the law. I've been arrested a few times for violence and driving offences, but it was all minor: a slap on the wrist, got community service or a fine. I've always had some struggles with the law, but at the same time, football has always been my passion, my job. When I did eventually get sentenced, I'd never been to a Crown Court before and it was all sort of new for me. To get sent to jail had a big impact, a massive wake up call. I had a good lifestyle. I was quite privileged to do the job I was doing, and I got sentenced to four years and four months.

My career, when I look back, and I'm still playing now, having had some successes and some failures, but going to jail, that first six months was really hard. I didn't really know anyone and kept my head down. Looking back, being in closed conditions was really hard, but when I got to go to Prescoed (and it was either Prescoed or Layhill) and it was a blessing to go there even though Layhill was virtually on my doorstep, you see. I talked to my wife, I wanted to go to Layhill, but the prison were saying go to Prescoed because there was a bus going there. Looking back it was definitely a blessing in disguise. I was able to get more ROTLs and there was a football team there as well. Looking back, it links in now because the opportunity to play a bit of football was good for me as I was coming up to the last year of my sentence. I planned to go back into football when I came out, so it was an opportunity to stay fit, do a lot of gym and get a lot of ROTL.

The first six months I struggled being away from the missus; going to jail was horrendous for me. I'd played for a lot of clubs and had a lot of success. At times, I'd probably underachieved and sometimes perhaps overachieved. Professional football is like that at times, a lot of ups and down; it's a very ruthless business. I played in every division of the Football League apart from the Premiership. I played in the Championship all the way through to Conference South, all sorts of levels of football. Had some good managers, some good coaches and some good experiences. At the same time, I've had some low moments, like when you're not playing. It becomes a week to week, up and down football journey, but at the same time it does toughen you up.

I got a lot of home leaves and I was able to work out. I came out in the June, and that's when pre-season started, so immediately I was talking to clubs, doing bleep tests every other day, training on a Wednesday and playing games on a Saturday. For me personally it was ideal for me to get back into football, so when I came out I was straight into a pre-season and ready to go. I did struggle a bit when the season started, being away for two years with the increased training and faster tempo of the games, but it was good.

I knew Prescoed had a team before I came because a lot of people talked about it. I did as much research as I could, but you don't actually know what to believe until you are there. But I know now why it was good that I went there. It helped me massively, like just being able to play football on grass! When I was in closed conditions in Guys Marsh there was a period where I didn't touch a football for six months. They had low staff levels and they weren't able to put on a five-a-side. They had other problems to deal with, people on the roof, people on strike; it was hell sometimes. I couldn't do anything really. I had to do what I could in the gym. It was so frustrating.

At Prescoed, we had a good team spirit. When I first went there, like a lot of the lads, I didn't know anyone, so the football was a real positive. Getting lads to do bleep tests, training hard. We dominated that league and they are still dominating teams now.

Looking back, there were guys there who took it professionally, who weren't taking the micky and stuff. We had a couple of bad eggs, but we were trying to do things professionally and I think a lot of the other teams respected that. Teams would tell us they'd had more problems with other teams than with us, people from a jail!

There were a couple of lads who played for the other teams in the league who knew I'd played for Newport, so word spread because I had a good spell there. A few of us were trying to go back there after release. I did have an opportunity to go back on trial, but they didn't offer me a contract at the time. Eastleigh did, and I knew it was too good to turn down. Looking back, I'll never close the door on Newport. I know the manager, he's doing really well at the moment, and he's being linked with other clubs too.

I was in a fairly unique position compared to a lot of other people in prison because football had been my job. Playing in jail, it definitely built my character because you get tested at times, so you have to learn patience. When I got sentenced I thought it was the end of my career and I was going to come out at thirty. That was always playing on my mind, I never knew if I would play again. Even before prison I've always done a lot of reading and a lot of educating myself for when I do retire or for coaching. So, in that sense, it woke me up. I knew I wouldn't be able to play forever. More of the lower league players will have to work again after retirement anyway, so I just made the most of my time, really.

As good as the football was at Prescoed, the standard is what it is and it's a lot lower than I was used to, so it took a while to adjust, really. The boys I played with, they're a good bunch of lads, and I still chat to a few of them now they're out. Through my contacts, I managed to get one lad some trials in Chippenham and Gloucester, but for him they just were too far away because he lives in Swansea. There's a couple of other lads that play in the Welsh League now. We had a good little team spirit, which helps, because it gets your mind off other worries and a lot of the lads need that. Looking back on it, in that way, it was the best thing I could have done. Layhill didn't have a football team and they don't have a lot of ROTL, so it could have been very different. It could have affected everything, but you don't realise [that] at the time.

When I came out I signed for Eastleigh with a one-year contract. It was hard, going back into that environment, being quite fearful of training, being worried about them judging me on my past. It wasn't easy, but I've been in that situation before. It took time to get going and I didn't get my first goal until November. It was really hard to settle into the game, and being a striker that's how you are judged. After a while, I scored some goals, but then I was out the team. At one point I thought I was going to have to give it in, but then I played again, scored, and had a really good run. I got player of the month the last two months of the season and finished joint top goal scorer. So I managed to get another year's contract at Eastleigh. It's not always been easy, but I'm always a fighter and willing to prove people wrong.

I was fearful at first, but it was more the anxiety because I'd been away for so long. Plus, I was getting a bit older, I was thirty years old and I was thinking, am I still the player I was? Have they signed a player from two years ago? When I got sentenced I was playing for Newport County at the time and I was doing well. They are a good football club in the league and I'd dropped down a division. You don't know how you are going to get on. Whenever you go to a new club, you're always going to lose some games, but you just want to score some goals and get a good run in the team. There's a couple of times where I'd not believe the amount of times I hit the post or missed the goal!

The football helped me to adapt to when I was released. I've always thought I had good ability, but I do remember the first pre-season game where I played away at Basingstoke and I was a bit rusty. It took a while because it was the first game I played in two and a half years. I remember I was a bit anxious before that, but once I got going I was confident that I'd be up and running in no time. I was maybe a bit rusty, mentally and physically, which is maybe why it took me a while to score my first goal.

I knew of players who had previously come in and out of prison and I've seen other players it's happened to as well. So I always used to look out for players that had gone to jail and use them as an example. You've got to keep yourself fit because nobody will sign you if you come out and you've put on weight. Even now I still have to prove myself now at Eastleigh. Sometimes people bring up the past, and the fans can be fickle at times, but you've just got to prove them wrong and that's what I intend to do.

If I hadn't played at Prescoed I think it would have taken me a lot longer to get up to speed than it did. I would have kept fit, and I do look after myself, and to be honest, in jail, you can't really binge eat! But a few of the lads I'd played with would have a curry every Saturday night. We'd cook it in the microwave, so you put yourself on a good diet. Looking back now, it could have been a different outcome, but I still think I would have been able to play, just maybe not at that high a standard as I am at Eastleigh. It might have taken me longer, but I think people would still have given me a chance because I did have a good career. I think teams are always looking for strikers to score goals.

Football in prison, I think it's a great release. I know a lot of lads, when I was in closed conditions, who when they couldn't go to the gym they'd get very anxious, they'd want to let off some steam because some lads have long sentences or problems at home. It's a good release for them. That release, and the endorphins and hormones, it definitely takes you away mentally from your surroundings. It's a good distraction and it makes you feel good about yourself physically. There were loads of lads that did gym and jog around on Saturdays around Prescoed doing laps, and this one guy, he used to do fifty laps! I think three and a half laps is a mile. It was their sort of drug, their release. You would finish your workout, come back in your cell and you knew you'd worked hard. By the time you got your head on the pillow, you'd feel good about yourself.

Undefeated

John felt it more than most. "I don't understand it? How the fuck can they turn us over like that? We battered them for ninety minutes and yet we couldn't score more than once? What the fuck!" His red shirt was thrown into the middle of the room, the number seven barely legible from the mud and grass stains that covered all his kit. His frustration matched his tackling and intensity in a central midfield role. He struggled to take his boots off with hands shaking from the experience. Fingers clawing at rain soaked laces. As Captain, he would always be the last one to leave the game behind.

John looked down at the floor. Searching for an answer that had passed. Paul, the other senior player and an ex-pro, had seen it all before. He spoke up. "John, you're right. We were all over them. Two shitty goals, both headers. That fat fuck as well, how did he get his head on it? We got to be first to it, clear your lines. We'll do them the next game. We'll batter them and score a ton of goals." Other players nodded and murmured in agreement.

Calum spoke up, which was rare. He wasn't having the criticism pointed at the defence for conceding from headers. "Thing is boys, if we didn't keep giving away stupid free kicks in the middle of the park, they wouldn't have scored, see? Every fucking time we got the ball every cunt would bomb forward wanting to score and we kick it long. Then we lose the ball and they're on the break. You've got to keep your shape boys. Play football. That's how we win these games."

One of the quietest on and off the pitch, Calum had an ally in his fellow defender Tom. "You know we got fuck all off the ref. You can't go in trying to take the man out as well. The ref's looking to give it and all their lot on the side will shout for anything. They've come off there looking like they won the fucking cup final."

"Too right. Fucking high fivin' each other they was. What's that all about? It's not fucking Premier League," chipped in Neil.

John quickly stood up to his six foot plus height and wide frame of muscle and tattoo. He was furious and hurt in equal measure. The loss still carried in the adrenaline coursing through his blood stream. He held a boot in one hand and shin pad in the other, using both to illustrate his point aggressively. Neil, chilled from vaping outside the changing room, was also bare chested, his strong tattooed torso emphasising his commitment to both strength and fitness. The two locked eyes and their team mates looked down. Neither was to be trifled with. The ball boys, normally full of wise cracks and banter, like Saturday court jesters, knew better than to get in the way. Instead, they craned their heads round the door to see what was unfolding. The two prisoners had the hardened experience of at least five prison sentences between them and were clearly a match for anyone, if it came to that. But everyone in the changing room knew that it wouldn't.

Still, Neil had poked at John's pride and so he replied. "I wait all fucking week for this game. I know it ain't Premier League but it's about pride. You got to do it on the pitch. Our fucking heads went down and they think they're better than us. We've got to do it in training on a Tuesday and we've got to fucking do it here in the games. In the summer there's twenty, thirty boys up here wanting to play. Today we had the bare eleven. That's fucking shit! No wonder they turned us over. What the fuck! I'll go round them up for next week. I'm not having it." He sat down to struggle with his second boot. Neil went back out for a vape. There was nowhere to sit anyway.

Watching it all from the side, the PEO, Mr Snape, stepped forward. Experienced and understanding of the men's characters, now was the right time to interject. The air was clearer. His words of calm reassurance were listened to by each player and sowed the seeds of recovery for the return fixture, which Prescoed won seven nil. For the rest of the season the team remained undefeated.

Deprived of their liberty, Prescoed FC's players were unable to do their arguing over tactics and dodgy decisions in the car home or down the pub after the game. The Officer understood the importance of the men having their say and blowing off, even if it got a little heated, to get it out of them. By the time they went back to their cells in twos and threes thirty minutes later, each player was in a better frame of mind and there would be no incidents that night in the prison.

Prescoed FC had just lost their first game in three years.

In any football club in the land, the changing room is a place of preparation before the game takes place and afterwards; it is a place of reflection on how the game went. The manager, coach or captain gives instructions on how the game should be played before a team leaves and the game starts. No team leaves the changing room with a plan to fail. The tactics and instructions imparted to the players are always intended to result in a successful performance over the next ninety minutes.

When the players return, whatever the result during the course of the match, the discussions between the players themselves or with the coach or manager, are reflective and directive in equal measure. The game is picked apart and successful moments celebrated. Equally, failures are remembered, interpreted and analysed to understand their root cause. A missed tackle here, a poor pass there; that's where their goal came from. The point of this reflective process is simple; it is to ensure that the same mistakes do not happen again. So that for the next game everything will go well. At least that is the plan.

Prescoed FC's home changing room is a box measuring no more than twenty feet by twenty feet, with benches on only two sides that cannot seat all the players at once. Instead they often get changed before and after games in instalments. But before games, when all the players are in at one time, it is impossible not to feel the intensity that comes from being in the presence of more than a dozen large, physically imposing men in close proximity, all listening intently to their captain and coach, and each determined to assert their footballing and physical dominance over their opposition. When one remembers that some of the players have previously been involved in acts of extreme violence, that intensity is taken up several notches.

In contrast, the atmosphere in the changing room after a game is one of celebration and elation. Goals are remembered through rose-tinted glasses where at least ten yards are added to every shot on goal from distance by the scorer. Everyone is happy they have won again. Jokes fly around and the loud, colourful banter of men in a football changing room lets you know that today in the prison, it was a good day. The contemplations and reflections take place later on in the evening, over a game of pool or the X Box, between the players, not in the changing room. Prescoed are undefeated; so any mistakes are forgotten about. Usually.

The one game where Prescoed lost for the first time in three years was as much a shock to the players as it was to the prison staff who found out about it on Monday. "Prescoed always win, don't they?"

The raw account of how that rare loss was felt and processed by the players, at the beginning of this chapter, and how they dealt with disappointment was an insight into how football is more than just a game at Prescoed. Overseen by a Prison Officer, the men blew off steam and immediately started blaming each other. To the casual observer it might have looked like a fight was going to break out, but the ability of football to help these prisoners with their behaviour was clear. They talked it out between themselves.

Even though the air was blue and the swear count was going up and up that was as far as it went.

The importance of sport in tackling anger management in particular should not be underestimated. According to the Ministry of Justice, in the twelve months to March 2019 there were over 34,000 incidents of violence and assault in prisons across England and Wales.[9] In Prescoed during this time there were only three.[10] In Prescoed, football is designed specifically to tackle this and several of the players understand that football helps them to stick to the rules and to deal with problems on the pitch. Despite provocation sometimes from the opposition, they understand that it is important to remain calm and not to respond with violence. The importance of self-control and not being aggressive is recognised by all the players. They see that they have more to lose by responding poorly to a foul or bad tackle. By sticking to the rules of the prison, the laws of the game and rules the staff put down (putting kit away, turning up at a certain time, etc.) Prescoed's footballers are getting a triple whammy.

Football not only helps the players with anger management, it also helps with other areas of their development, such as the social aspects of their personality like developing their communication and motivation skills. Several players talk about how football helps to build character, especially for the younger players who might feel overawed coming into the prison. Crucially, it helps to teach them to understand right from wrong and this helps to show how football can have such a positive impact on the players, even though they will only be at Prescoed for a matter of months before they are released.

Prison can often be a selfish place, especially in closed conditions, and some men when they arrive at Prescoed still retain this aspect to their character. In closed conditions, prisoners talk about having to look after themselves and be guarded about what they share. In open conditions, this attitude starts to be eroded and is replaced by a sense of trust. All the players have been assessed not only to be suitable to serve time in a Category D prison; they have also been assessed as suitable to play football. Any open prison has minimal security and many prisoners spend their day away from the prison on licence to carry out work or participate in education. They only house prisoners that have been risk-assessed and deemed suitable for open conditions. Football is an extension of the trust present in an open prison.

The pitch, however, is the living and breathing embodiment of the trust present in HMP Prescoed, especially its location. To the players who have been in prison for many years at a time, the fact that you cannot see the prison or any HMPPS signage while you are pitch-side is a significant step and it is not lost on them. The players all talk about feeling like they are on a cup final pitch or playing back home; anywhere but playing in a prison. The opposition also reinforces this perception and emphasises again the trust that they are presented with. They aren't playing against other prisoners. Instead, they are playing against the sort of teams and the sort of men in the type of communities that they themselves have come from.

If you imagine a British prison, it's likely to be like the ones you may see on TV. Several landings on top of each other converging to a central point, overseen by Prison Officers. Their design is based loosely on the panopticon design where there is a central tower surrounded by cells on all sides, overseen by a sentry or watchman. The assumption of the panopticon design is that the people in the cells are always being watched, because they cannot see the sentry themselves and so adhere to the rules and behave. The theory of the design is that it provides a form of self-policing in this way. Nowadays the Prison Officer as a central sentry is not quite replaced but certainly backed-up by surveillance cameras.

The panopticon idea comes from Jeremy Bentham, a renowned philosopher and social reformer of the late eighteenth and early nineteenth centuries. Although he never lived to see one built, he took the idea of a panopticon prison to the Prime Minister of the day, William Pitt the Younger, who commissioned a study into the feasibility of developing a *National Penitentiary*, as it was called.[11] The French philosopher Michel Foucault popularised Bentham's panopticon idea in the 1970s when he argued that it may be used to illustrate how discipline-based societies can subjugate its citizens, such as through CCTV [12], because you don't know when you are being watched.[13] Interestingly, in his later years, Bentham spoke against his own panopticon idea and instead argued for a system where an individual was questioned as a means of being held to account. This is very similar to the process of restorative justice, which is a common way of helping those affected by a crime, including the perpetrators, to repair the damage that has been caused and be able to move on.

Of course, the prisoners in Prescoed are usually within the last two years of their sentences and will have undergone numerous rehabilitative courses and programmes to get them to the status of a Category D prisoner. But the idea of a place for prisoners within a prison environment, where they are made to feel like they are not in a prison, is about as far from the panopticon idea as you can go. This is what the football pitch at Prescoed represents to the prisoners there and it is undoubtedly a contributory factor to an acknowledged and fundamentally successful institution, delivering its key responsibilities very well according to its 2018 Inspection Report.[14]

Several panopticon prisons were built in the Netherlands and the USA. Although the intention of the panopticon design was supposed to encourage self-reflection, Foucault argued that instead the design benefitted a more surveillance and discipline based system which instead crushed individuality or individual freedom, to the detriment of anything approaching rehabilitation.

A recent study into the role of prison design emphasised the importance of prison architecture, analysing the design, floor plans and living conditions of over thirty prisons in the Netherlands.[15] The report focussed mainly on the importance of staff-prisoner relationships and suggested that 'campus' style prisons, which appear to be very close in design to Prescoed, create the best environment for fostering these positive relationships. The 'campus' prisons aim to create a 'homely' atmosphere where communal activities take place, prisoners are treated humanely, and there is a strong focus on rehabilitation. Small communal living units also helped facilitate more personal staff-prisoner interactions.

Interestingly, the report also acknowledged that often it is the prison staff who actually feel more at ease with panopticon or surveillance based prisons, allowing them to see in an instant where any potential threat may come from. Yet, from a prisoner's perspective, it appears that open facilities support positivity while panopticon designed institutions support negativity.

This approach is clearly part of a process that is working. In fact, recently, several prisons in the Netherlands were closed because of their low crime rate, whereas in the UK nearly half of adults are reconvicted within one year of release from prison![16] The benchmark of open style prisons is Norway's Bastoy prison with a reoffending rate of just 16%, which may be attributed its island location, its community-based approach, and the 'social worker' approach of it prison officers.[17]

The living conditions and design of Prescoed clearly play a part in the rehabilitation of prisoners, including the location of its football pitch, as well the encouragement of men going to work or participating in education during the final stages of their sentence. All of these activities seem to represent a step towards leading a 'normal life' away from crime. To those in the team, this is what football represents too.

Throughout their sentences, whether in open or closed conditions, football plays the part of something the men did when they were younger, such as at school, or it represents freedom. It seems to be a place where they are focussed on the game and the competition and forget about where they actually are. As one player explained, "Football, they can't take that away from you." It also represents an area of choice in a place where being deprived of one's liberty comes with the removal of the ability to make personal decisions. In closed conditions especially, the regime is designed so that one size fits all and personal adaptations and desires are rarely accommodated. In Prescoed, almost the first thing that the players do is get brightly coloured boots sent to them from a mail order catalogue or from family, rather than wear the prison issue Hummel black ones. They are beginning to express and rediscover their ability to make personal choices again.

Football at Prescoed doesn't just represent something done previously. It also represents a future for the players, such as wanting to play for a team again when released or the possibility to study the sport academically at university. In this way football continues to be a thread that runs through their life before, during and after their sentence. Nowhere is this more evident than with the experience of players who recognise their own USP where they could talk to young people or adults who might have been in trouble with the police previously, but who still play and love sport. Their 'lived experience' of crime, conviction and sentence is regularly used as being an important component of using the experiences of those who have been where others might follow in order to break a destructive cycle of behaviour.[18]

Football has long been used to combat problematic issues in society. Activities such as the Homeless World Cup or anti-knifecrime all-star matches are effective at raising awareness and bringing partners together to help tackle some of these problems.[19] At Prescoed, football plays a part in the rehabilitation of the players. Although, on a cold and rainy Saturday afternoon on a boggy pitch, where it appears the only thing that matters is to win, it's hard to remember that's what the game is there for. Allowing the footballers to play in the community: participating in Gwent Central Division Two is part of the prison's process of reducing reoffending. Whether the league see it that way isn't clear, but they should be applauded for supporting Prescoed FC's participation in the various guises the league has gone through for over twenty years.

The good disciplinary record of Prescoed as a prison is reflected in that of the Prescoed football team. The number of red or yellow cards received by players appears to be quite low. The prison itself isn't a place where you feel unsafe, despite the fact there is a high concentration of people who have broken the law within your vicinity; some quite significantly. Prisoner football teams in film or in print may be portrayed as being overtly physical, violent even, but this is not the case at Prescoed. Several players and staff noted that just to play the men have to abide by three sets of rules: those of the prison, those of the staff, and the laws of the game. This is before any consideration of tactics or team selection to win a game.

To the players the effect on them of this triple whammy of rules is that it teaches them self-control, especially in the face of perceived or actual provocation, which may come from the opposition, a team member or even a referee. In fact, in the face of provocation, several of the players state that it pushes them to try harder to win the game, rather than react. They talk about 'biting their tongue', 'learning to be calm' or behaving in 'a calm and controlled manner'. There is an acknowledgement that the players as individuals are a part of something that matters to them and they do not want to lose the opportunity to play football, as they understand it could easily affect not only their chances of playing, but also increase the likelihood of being sent back to closed conditions, to another prison. Back to square one.

Allied to the role of helping them improve their behaviour, the players realise they are part of a team. Being part of a team often can mean putting one's personal considerations aside for the team performance to be optimized. This is certainly a common theme for the players at Prescoed, where the players realise that they need to come together as a team to get results. When you understand that the team can change in an instant with new players coming into the jail or prisoners being released midway through the season, then this would be a challenge for any team in any league.

Perhaps because a lot of the players have played before or perhaps as a result of the prison environment, you can see people pulling together as a team both on and off the pitch. The outcome of the passionate and heated discussion at the start of this chapter was that Prescoed were undefeated for the remainder of the season. Each Saturday, several non-footballers come to act as ball boys and *de facto* supporters at every game. Alan takes pride in ensuring that the kit is washed after each game and hangs the shirts up on their pegs on Saturday mornings. Joe, who had been waiting for a while to play up front, went in goal with no questions asked when the goalkeeper was injured early in a game. Sam asks every new arrival at the prison if they can play football and explains how to get involved. Paul, the ex-pro, quietly encourages the younger new players who are nervous about playing to get the best out of them. John spends all week checking to make sure the players are ready for Saturday. All these actions are those of people who want their team to win.

Sam's seniority, his easy-going demeanour, and his friendliness belied his status as a first-time prisoner and Induction Orderly. He would ask everyone coming through the unit if they played football and to what standard. Several players came to training and match days directly as a result of his intervention. His impact especially is symptomatic of the role football plays at Prescoed. Working as an Orderly, he welcomed newly arrived prisoners to where they stay for their first night, before being allocated a more permanent room in one of ten accommodation units. Officially the purpose of Induction is to inform prisoners about prison life, the regime and their responsibilities and privileges, and to begin to prepare them for their return to the community. This may include information on Chaplaincy, Healthcare (if individuals need access to medication for example), Samaritans, Listeners, Disability Services, and much more. It doesn't necessarily say anything about football, but to Sam catching people early was all part of being a member of the team.

As a first-time prisoner Sam was acutely aware of the need to grasp hold of anything that would help new arrivals adjust to Prescoed and open conditions. Although several players knew each other from local prisons, for those who didn't, football might play an important role in helping them settle in. It helped them meet others and in a short space of time they might have a circle of friends of up to fifteen people. This was important, not only to help fit in, but also to ask people how to do something or where to go, for example. This is especially important in open conditions because the onus is very much on you in terms of how to structure your day. In closed conditions the day is already structured for you and you simply go along with it. At Prescoed, you have to think for yourself which, if you have spent a long time in a closed prison, may well be a struggle to adjust to at first. The weekly cycle of Tuesday training and Saturday games gives an illusion of structure, but there are still a lot of other hours in the day to fill.

Football also helped the time to pass more quickly, especially when combined with the frequency of games. Several players were able to count down their sentences by looking at the fixture list. They would keep Saturdays for football and Sundays for family visits which, when combined with work during the week on or off camp, helped their sentences pass more quickly for them.

The appeal of football to the players is a mixture of love for the game and the opportunity to keep fit. In any prison the gym is a focal point for a lot of male prisoners, which is the same at Prescoed. For some of the footballers they acknowledge that the game plays a part in their weekly workouts, such as by giving them an extra aerobic fitness session. For these players, they would regularly top up their training with a session after the game in the gym to give themselves a full body workout.

This attention to physical fitness unsurprisingly gave the players a significant edge over their competitors and was a reason they felt they won so many games, and it's hard to disagree. Added to this the players are without things like beer and takeaway food that they acknowledge was a big part of their lives before prison. Deprived of these distractions and many others, the players jump head first into physical fitness and healthy eating to fill the void. For some, such as Balley, this sobriety helps them get their focus back to where they were before drugs took hold and they started on a path into prison. For others, like Alex, Neil, and John, there is a clear distinction being made that healthy body equals healthy mind, in terms of their plans for a crime-free life after prison. No one plans to return to prison of course.

The role of sport and exercise can mean more than just plans for rehabilitation, because there is a clear link between prison and mental health. The statistics show that 16% of men receive treatment for a mental health problem in the year before arrest. 15% of men in prison reported symptoms of psychosis, whereas the rate among the general public is about 4%. Self-inflicted deaths such as suicide are 8.6 times more likely in prison than in the general population. Of this group, 70% of people who died in prison had already been identified as having mental health needs.[20] One report even suggests that over 90% of prisoners have a mental disorder in England and Wales, citing the prison environment and the rules and regimes governing daily life inside prison as being seriously detrimental to mental health.[21] For a sense of comparison with the non-prison population, Mind – the mental health charity, report approximately 25% of people in England and Wales need mental health support in an average year.[22]

The link between playing football and improved mental health over and above the period spent actually playing, such as a sixty or ninety minute game, show that improvements do occur on a longer term basis. Research on both playing and watching football suggests mental health benefits are generated from being part of a supportive group that itself generates a feeling of warmth, purpose and social inclusion.[23] In other words, it is both being part of the team and sharing a common goal, such as to win games and win the league, which helps promote positive mental health, both for the players and supporters. At Prescoed, the game helped to improve both the players' mood and the mood of the prison as a whole, when the team did well.

All the players talked about football helping them with the stress of being a prisoner. The game helped to relieve tension and other anxieties such as family problems that could negatively affect their mental health. Of all the players, Daniel's experience particularly highlighted how football played a part in his mental health journey. Suffering PTSD from his experiences in Afghanistan, being forced out of the army, a relationship breakdown and serving a prison sentence; each of these circumstances would test even those with the strongest mental health. Football was playing a part to help him get off medication and become stronger, both physically and mentally.

The *healthy body, healthy mind* approach from the players is backed up by a study showing that improvements in footballers' mental health can also prompt broader improvements in personal health. It also called for more mainstream acknowledgement of these links and called for more support to be made available.[24] Interestingly, in the season that this project took place, the English Football League launched the #OnYourSide campaign with Mind, to raise awareness of mental health and to improve the approach to mental health in football.[25] Every player's shirt in the league carried the Mind logo next to their name on the back, the first time a charity was used in this way by the league.

The description of Prescoed from its senior staff is that is a working prison and a lot of its population are employed in various jobs within the jail to help it function, such as cleaning, catering, recycling and more. The rest are off camp on work placements giving the men valuable work experience, and crucially some money in their pocket, designed to set them up for when they are released. Whilst there are plenty of staff at Prescoed in a variety of prison officer and civilian roles, they are not as visible as they would be in a closed prison. There is significantly less escorting of visitors through locked doors to corridors flanked by burley, silent security staff, which is the norm in any Cat B or Cat C. In fact, at Prescoed, it is often difficult to distinguish between prisoner and staff member. Often it is only the uniform or gender which helps.

With such a different staffing model, the impression given is that the prison is less for punishment and more for preparation. The departments dealing with education, resettlement and employment all realise that they are the last stop before release. Subsequently, good prisoner-staff relationships help to forge the bonds needed to prepare for life back out in the community after release.

The role of the four PE Staff running football at Prescoed is a curious mixture of manager, coach, father figure(s) and councillor probably unlike much else in the prison system. Each Saturday, the team that the Officer puts out, although intended to win, is also there to help the men start to take responsibility for themselves and their activity. The players fill up the water bottles, pump up the balls, get the kit ready and in some cases sort out disagreements between themselves. Egos are not massaged, especially of the most talented individuals. If they are not prepared to do their time on the bench, then they will not be selected. Where disputes occur, the players are encouraged to resolve them between themselves, as a process of conflict resolution and problem solving. The staff know the players are a long way from being the angry young men who they were, perhaps when first arrested.

The freedom of expression is not one way, as the players are prisoners and understand where a line may be that they must not cross. The colourful banter between players exists like it does in any sports team and the experienced PE Staff join in with many a line used to raise a smile and cut a player down to size, should they need it. But rarely is it returned by a player towards an officer, perhaps because they are unsure of the repercussions or anxious about not being selected. Instead, the name calling and jokes are directed inwards by the players most of the time.

The players talk about having a different type of relationship with the PE Staff at Prescoed, one based on mutual respect. That relationship appears to be different to other staff-prisoner relationships in the prison. In some cases they are seen as 'father figures', to whom players will go for advice. The staff joke that their office is sometimes used like a surrogate psychologist's office.

Tucked away at the top of the camp where the perma-smell of years of accumulated sports equipment and kit permeates the fabric of the building, the PE department fits the bill of a safe space for somewhere to go to talk about something on your mind. It is away from the management offices of the prison and behind the gym, at the top of the camp, so it is easy to sit and talk away from any disruption, intrusion or observation. Conversations range from football to relationships to families to the future and all points in between. For the players it provides a place of relative confidentiality to talk with staff who have that everyday detached link with the outside world that their fellow prisoners don't have, without the emotional ties of family conversations. For those men who grew up without a father in their life, these are the sort of conversations with a father figure that, arguably, if they had had access to earlier in their life, may not have led them to prison or crime.

In fact the link to football and family goes beyond the absence of father figures. Perhaps because of this, several players were determined to support their children playing football too, once they were released. The family day, for example, was an opportunity for partners and relatives – and crucially children – to connect with their father by watching them play football. Often players were unavailable for matches because of home leave. Even though the team provided a form of surrogate family, in terms of camaraderie, which was important and positive, a player's family was an even bigger draw, one of the few to trump football in the prison.

The numerous theories and interventions around rehabilitation can underpin lots of programmes designed to break the cycle of reoffending. Addressing issues like drug and alcohol abuse, anger management, and more all have their part in the prison system and play a valuable role in helping some people to change their life, to live a life away from crime. For some, these programmes work and work well. But for others, the opportunity to talk person to person, to explore conversations in a non-judgemental arena, which you can return to again and again, is the most valuable. Men who either by accident, because of the fractured families they were born into, or the communities they grew up in of low aspiration, unemployment and deprivation, they may never have had the opportunity to sit and reflect, talk and ask for advice.

Football at Prescoed works for a number of reasons, some by design and some by good fortune. The normality that surrounds it is the very thing that draws people to it because it is not the norm in the prison estate and so it feels outside of regular prison activities. This outlier status means it's not quite prison and, because they cannot be promoted or relegated, it's not quite league football, either. The team changes week by week each season, so they're not quite a club. The pitch is away from the camp so it's not quite prison. Football, rather than being reflective of any individual policy or Prison Service Order, has become something greater than the sum of its parts. To paraphrase Bill Shankly, football at Prescoed isn't just a game; it's something far more important than that.

Final League Table, Season 2018/19

Gwent Central League Division 2

Teams	P	W	D	L	GD	Pts
Prescoed	16	14	1	1	123	43
Race	16	11	1	4	33	34
Mardy	16	10	2	4	14	32
Usk Town	16	8	0	8	-5	24
Pontypool Town	16	6	2	8	-10	20
Blaenavon Blues	16	6	1	9	-16	19
Forgeside	16	6	0	10	-20	18
Pontnewynydd	16	5	1	10	-23	16
Bailey Rangers	16	2	0	14	-96	6

Acknowledgements

This book would not have happened without a whole host of people supporting me. It is only right to thank them all here by giving them a little mention. In no particular order, they are as follows. Neville Southall for his support and the contribution of the Foreword to this book. Adrian Clark for the use of his recording equipment and interest in this project. Sam Ellis for transcribing the interviews so accurately. Russell Todd of Indycube and Podcast Pêl-Droed respectively, who were instrumental in securing the research grant for this project. Jaime Fitzgerald of Fitz Design for the excellent cover design work. Clare Lloyd, Pwyll ap Stifin and Iva Gray of Prisoners Education Trust for getting me into Prescoed initially, plus Hannah Richards for her criminology literature suggestions. Chris Leslie for technical advice and accuracy. Dave Rowe at the FAW for his memories of the Wales training sessions at Prescoed. Dr Justine Reilly of Sporting Heritage whose funding support made this project happen. Leon Barton for his very useful advice for a first time author. David Collins of Welsh Football magazine for all the background information on Prescoed's performances through the years. Prof Rosie Meek for her input into the design and concept of the project, research approval suggestions and comprehensive research into sport and criminal justice. Prof Amanda Kirby and Prof Kirstine Szifris for support and suggestions on gaining this project's research approval. Dr Mark Crane for his patient support in helping me secure this project's approval with HMPPS in Wales. Governor Giles Mason for allowing this project to happen, even though he felt it was the wrong shaped ball! Dai West for his insight into football at Prescoed and links to the Welsh national squad. Mark Lewis of Prescoed for ensuring that this project ran smoothly. Each of the PE Officers, Ian Moore, Mark Harrison, Gareth Davies and Gordon Snape, for allowing me to attend training sessions, run the line on a Saturday, sit in the changing rooms and participate as fully as possible. All the teams, players and officials that make up Gwent Central Division Two and played at Prescoed throughout the season. The many staff at Prescoed who played their part in booking interview rooms, getting me through security and generally tolerating my weekly presence. Each of the players interviewed and all the others who may not have been part of this project but were a member of the team or supported on a Saturday. Many of you didn't realise I wasn't a prisoner which I'll take as a research compliment! A huge thank you to my editor Dr Chris Dennis for his support, attention to detail and positivity, all whilst supporting the Villa during a very challenging season – thank you Chris. My wife Annie for her unending patience and support throughout this year-long project. Finally anyone who I may have forgotten to include in this list, consider yourself thanked here also.

Notes

[1] Home Office (1946) *Report of the Commissioners of Prisons and Directors of Convict Prisons for the Year 1945*. London: HMSO.

[2] Sturge, G. (2019) *UK Population Statistics* (Commons Library Briefing Paper Number CBP-04334). 23 July 2019. Available at: https://researchbriefings.parliament.uk/ResearchBriefing/Summary/SN04334#fullreport Accessed 30 August 2019.

[3] Home Office (1965) *Report on the Work of the Prison Department 1964*. London: HMSO.

[4] Meek, R. (2018) *A Sporting Chance An Independent Review of Sport in Youth and Adult Prisons*. London: HMSO.

[5] Jones, J. (2018) 'HMP Prescoed', *Welsh Football: The National Football Magazine of Wales*, 208, n.p.

[6] Welsh Government (2014) *Wales Reducing Reoffending Strategy 2014 – 2016*.

[7] Rowe, D. (2019) Email to Jamie Grundy, 6 September.

[8] Giggs, R. (2019) cited by Mora, L. (2019) [*Twitter*] 12 March 2019. Available at: https://twitter.com/Mora_sport/status/1105436833146642433 (Accessed: 30 August 2019).

[9] Ministry of Justice (2019) *Safety in Custody Statistics, England and Wales: Deaths in Prison Custody to March 2019; Assaults and Self-harm to December 2018*. Available at: https://assets.publishing.service.gov.uk/government/uploads/system/uploads/attachment_data/file/797074/safety-custody-bulletin-q4-2018.pdf (Accessed: 15 August 2019).

[10] Her Majesty's Inspectorate of Prisons and Estyn (2018) *Report on an unannounced inspection of HMP Usk and HMP & YOI Prescoed*. Available at: https://www.justiceinspectorates.gov.uk/hmiprisons/wp-content/uploads/sites/4/2018/02/Usk-and-Prescoed-Web-2017.pdf (Accessed: 15 August 2019).

[11] Semple, Janet (1993). Bentham's Prison: a Study of the Panopticon Penitentiary. Oxford: Clarendon Press.

[12] McMullan, T. (2015) 'What does the panopticon mean in the age of digital surveillance?' *The Guardian*, 23 July 2015. Available at: https://www.theguardian.com/technology/2015/jul/23/panopticon-digital-surveillance-jeremy-bentham Accessed: 30 August 2019.

[13] Foucault, M. (1977) *Discipline and Punish: The Birth of the Prison*. Translated by Alan Sheridan. London: Allen Lane.

[14] Her Majesty's Inspectorate of Prisons and Estyn (2018) *Report on an unannounced inspection of HMP Usk and HMP & YOI Prescoed*. Available at: https://www.justiceinspectorates.gov.uk/hmiprisons/wp-content/uploads/sites/4/2018/02/Usk-and-Prescoed-Web-2017.pdf (Accessed: 15 August 2019).

[15] Jacobs, R. (2017) 'How prison architecture can transform inmates' lives', *Pacific Standard*, 3 May. Available at: https://psmag.com/news/jail-prison-architecture-inmates-crime-design-82968 (Accessed: 15 August 2019).

[16] Prison Reform Trust (2018) *Prison: the facts. Bromley Briefings Summer 2018.* Available at: http://www.prisonreformtrust.org.uk/Portals/0/Documents/Bromley%20Briefings/Summer%202018%20factfile.pdf (Accessed: 15 August 2019).

[17] James, E. (2013) 'Bastoy: the Norwegian prison that works', *The Guardian*, 4 September. Available at: https://www.theguardian.com/society/2013/sep/04/bastoy-norwegian-prison-works (Accessed: 15 August 2019).

[18] Webster, R. (2017) 'Brendan's story: the importance of lived experience', *Russell Webster*, 26 August. Available at: http://www.russellwebster.com/brendan-turnaround/ (Accessed: 15 August 2019).

[19] Homeless World Cup Foundation (2019) *Who we are.* Available at: https://homelessworldcup.org/about/ (Accessed: 15 August 2019); de Peyer, R. (2018) 'Grime artists including Dappy and Kojo Funds line-up for anti-knife crime football match', *Evening Standard*, 26 June. Available at: https://www.standard.co.uk/news/london/grime-artists-including-dappy-and-kojo-funds-lineup-for-antiknife-crime-football-match-a3872586.html (Accessed: 15 August 2019).

[20] Prison Reform Trust (2019) *Mental health care in prisons.* Available at: http://www.prisonreformtrust.org.uk/WhatWeDo/Projectsresearch/Mentalhealth (Accessed: 15 August 2019).

[21] Birmingham, L. (2003) 'The mental health of prisoners', *Advances in Psychiatric Treatment*, 9, pp. 191-99.

[22] Mind (2017) *Mental Health Facts and Statistics.* Available at: https://www.mind.org.uk/media/34727125/facts-statistics-2017-pdf-version.pdf Accessed 30 August 2019.

[23] Heun, R. and Pringle, A. (2018) 'Football does not improve mental health: a systematic review on football and mental health disorders', *Global Psychiatry*, 1(1), pp. 25-37.

[24] McElroy, P., Evans, P. and Pringle, A. (2008) 'Sick as a parrot or over the moon: an evaluation of the impact of playing regular matches in a football league on mental health service users', *Practice Development in Health Care*, 7(1), pp. 40-48.

[25] Mind (2013) *We're on your side.* Available at: https://www.mind.org.uk/news-campaigns/campaigns/on-your-side/?ctaId=/about-us/our-policy-work/sport-physical-activity-and-mental-health/slices/efl-onyourside/ (Accessed: 15 August 2019).

Printed in Poland
by Amazon Fulfillment
Poland Sp. z o.o., Wrocław

50224417R00068